Experiencing
GOD
by
HIS NAMES

DICK PURNELL

HARVEST HOUSE PUBLISHERS
EUGENE, OREGON

Cover by Lucas Art and Design, Jenison, Michigan

EXPERIENCING GOD BY HIS NAMES
Copyright © 2015 Dick Purnell
Published by Harvest House Publishers
Eugene, Oregon 97402
www.harvesthousepublishers.com

Library of Congress Cataloging-in-Publication Data
Purnell, Dick.
Experiencing God by his names / Dick Purnell.
    pages cm
Includes bibliographical references and index.
ISBN 978-0-7369-2802-1 (pbk.)
ISBN 978-0-7369-4047-4 (eBook)
1. God—Name—Biblical teaching. 2. God (Christianity)—Name—Meditations 3. Devotional exercises. I. Title.
BT180.N2P869 2015
231'.4—dc23

2014042876

Printed in the United States of America

15 16 17 18 19 20 21 22 23 / BP-JH / 10 9 8 7 6 5 4 3 2 1

To God the Father.
This book is for You.
How I praise Your name that someday the
Son will hand everything over to You.

⁓

Then the end will come, when [Christ] hands over
the kingdom to God the Father
after he has destroyed
all dominion, authority and power.
1 Corinthians 15:24

Acknowledgments

To Christina Holder—You have been a joy to work with. Thank you for utilizing your excellent talents and gifts of editing and writing. You helped me conceive of this book and encouraged me to research and write what I was learning. My family is grateful for your friendship and delightful spirit.

To Joe Carlin, my good friend for over 20 years—I enjoy how you viewed this project and the vision you gave me to pursue my dream of sharing with people the excitement I feel about the myriad names of God. You helped me refocus when I hit some rough spots, and you were always challenging me to press on.

To Ed Bright—You are a warm and friendly computer genius. You made the complex database for this project work so smoothly and efficiently. This book would have been extremely more difficult to write if you had not stepped in to put your expertise to work designing and simplifying the process.

To my Thursday-morning men: Richard Hopkins, Joel Lueck, Dan Garguilo, Kerry Perkins, Mark Kloefkorn, Joe Carlin, Jim Bartley, Michael Hillan, Chris Rackley, John Schefke, and many others who have attended our gatherings over the last 14 years—Each week we've enthusiastically discussed the Bible and its impact on our lives. Your genuine insights and practical comments broadened my understanding of how God, through His names, relates to us each day. I love laughing together.

To Nick Harrison—Thanks for your strong encouragement. I offered to quit, and you told me to keep going. Your kind words were simply, "Go, Dick, go." Whoever reads this book and learns more about our wonderful Lord should thank you for motivating me to keep writing.

Contents

Introduction

When you meet someone new, what is the first thing you say? Usually, it's something like, "Hi, my name is…" How many names do you give? Probably two—first and last. Rarely, you might give three names—first, middle, and last. Or you may have a hyphenated first or last name or more than one middle name. How would you react if someone you just met introduced him- or herself by giving you *ten* names? While the person was saying all those names, you'd probably be thinking, "This is taking too much time!" or "I'll never remember all these names." If ten is too many, how would you react if the person responded by giving you more than 250 names? You'd probably be sorry you asked.

But if the Person is God, you'd want to hear all His names, wouldn't you? Sure you would! Each of God's names means something so significant that it gives you a glimpse of His magnificent character and the way He acts.

Unlike you and me, God's names weren't given to Him by someone else. No one looked in a book of baby names to choose which ones they liked so they could pick some nice names to give Him. God chose His own names. Your parents decided on your name; God chose names for Himself that reveal who He is and what He's like. Why? Because He wants us to know and understand Him and His ways. Our finite minds are so limited that we need a helpful way to comprehend the vast complexity of God's character and actions. So He chose each of His names to give us a window into Himself.

The huge array of God's names is like a mosaic. A mosaic is a beautiful picture or pattern made up of many small, individual pieces. Each one contains a small section of the whole picture. When you look closely at one piece, you see a little bit of color and maybe some lines. It looks pretty, but it's difficult to figure out what the whole mosaic will look like. Take a few steps back and gaze at the pieces of the mosaic. You can see more colors and lines that fit together, and you begin to notice a pattern. Step back again, and you see more pieces. The more you see, the more the gorgeous picture unfolds and the more you understand the intent of the artist. Likewise, each of God's names gives us insight into a part of His character and ways. The more names we know, the more we know about God and how He behaves. In fact, God reveals more than 250 of His names so that we can get to know and understand Him—as much as human beings can possibly comprehend a supreme, heavenly Being.

But knowledge of God is just the beginning of His desires for us. The more we learn about God through His names, the more we'll want to become like Him. And the more we want to become like Him, the harder we'll try—well, as much as any sinful human being can.

Though God reveals Himself through many names, each name doesn't refer to a different God. There is only *one* God; however, there are three Persons in the godhead or trinity: God the Father, God the Son, and God the Holy Spirit. You've heard some of their names already: Lord, Father, Jesus, Son, Christ, Savior, Holy Spirit, and so forth. But there are many more names God has chosen to use to reveal Himself to us.

For this book, I've chosen 140 of God's names for us to study. I believe that as you learn more about these unique names, you'll discover a much larger picture of who God is and your love for Him will deepen. So get ready for an exciting adventure into aspects of God few others know.

Translating God's Names

Before we dig in, let's consider this question: What is a "name"? For us humans, it's simply an identifier that separates us from others. For God, it's different. Each name has an important meaning. But picking out His names in the Bible isn't always so simple for two reasons.

First, various versions of the Bible translate the same Hebrew and Greek words differently. (The Old Testament was written in Hebrew; the New Testament was written in Greek.) Take, for example, John 15:26: "When the *Advocate* comes, whom I will send to you from the Father— the Spirit of truth who goes out from the Father—he will testify about me." The name "Advocate" used here is the translation of the Greek word *parakletos*. That's how the 2011 edition of New International Version translated the word. However, the same exact word in the 1984 New International Version was translated "Counselor." The King James Bible translates *parakletos* as "Comforter"; the New American Standard Bible translates it

12

as "Helper"; and the Message Bible translates it as "Friend." Five different words translated from the same original word! To minimize the confusion of various translations, I've chosen the 2011 New International Version for all the names found in this book. If you use a different translation of the Bible, it may use other names instead of the ones listed in this book. I encourage you to keep reading though. You'll learn a lot even if you use a different Bible as your "go to" version.

One other important note on translations. Throughout the Old Testament there are two distinctly different Hebrew words that are translated into the English word "Lord." Whenever you see the word LORD in small capitals, this is a translation of the Hebrew word *Yahweh*, which the Old Testament Jewish scholars changed to *Jehovah*. This is the most frequent name of God given in the Old Testament, and it appears more than 6,000 times. Another Hebrew word, *Adonai*, which means "master" or "owner," is also translated as "Lord." To differentiate these two Hebrew words, the translators designated *Adonai* as "Lord" with regular uppercase and lowercase letters. This difference, however, doesn't carry over into the New Testament. There's only one Greek word, *kurios,* that's translated "Lord."

Second, there are five *types* of names for God. It's helpful to understand the differences.

- *Type one*—personal names. These are names God calls Himself. For example, "Living One": "I am the Living One; I was dead, and now look, I am alive for ever and ever! And I hold the keys of death and Hades" (Revelation 1:18). "LORD" (English translation of *Yahweh* or *Jehovah*) is God's primary name to all generations (Exodus 3:15).

- *Type two*—possessive names. These names link one of God's names with a specific noun using the connector word "of." For example, "King of glory": "Lift up your heads, you gates; be lifted up, you ancient doors, that the *King of glory* may come in" (Psalm 24:7). God reigns and possesses the attribute of glory. Other possessive names include "God of Israel," "Lord of lords," and "Spirit of grace."

- *Type three*—descriptive names. These reveal characteristics or attributes about God, such as "Rock": "The LORD lives!

Praise be to my Rock! Exalted be my God, the Rock, my Savior!" (2 Samuel 22:47). God is not literally a rock, but He is *personified* as a rock because He has attributes like a rock—immovable, unchanging, strong. He uses the word as a description of one aspect of His character.

Other descriptive names connect an adjective to a noun that qualifies a particular aspect of God. He is called "Chief Shepherd": "And when the *Chief Shepherd* appears, you will receive the crown of glory that will never fade away" (1 Peter 5:4). Out of all the leaders and shepherds of people, God is preeminent over all of them. He is the chief one. Additional descriptive names are "Morning Star, "Lion of the tribe of Judah," and "true vine."

- *Type four*—symbolic names. These represent one of His qualities, such as "Prince of Peace": "To us a child is born, to us a son is given, and the government will be on his shoulders. And he will be called Wonderful Counselor, Mighty God, Everlasting Father, *Prince of Peace*" (Isaiah 9:6). He is like a prince over a kingdom. In this case, He is the ruler over the kingdom of peace, a symbol of His authority to bring peace and govern it. The Bible is filled with symbolic names, including "Lamb," "Word of God," "Overseer," and "Root of Jesse."

- *Type five*—ascribed names. People addressed God by these names. For example, God is called "Son of the Blessed One" by the chief priest: "Jesus remained silent and gave no answer. Again the high priest asked him, 'Are you the Messiah, the Son of the Blessed One?'" (Mark 14:61). Jesus certainly was the Son of God. The chief priest asked that question to goad Jesus into incriminating Himself so the religious leaders could get evidence of blasphemy (an ordinary human claiming to be God).

These five types help us get a clearer picture of the vast mosaic of God's magnificent character. Each name gives us a greater understanding of how superb and complex our Lord is.

God Reveals His Names in a Progression

One of the main features of this book is that the names you'll read about are given in chronological order. The Bible wasn't written chronologically; it was written in sections. The Old Testament has 39 "books" in it, and they are presented in different categories. The first five books of the Bible (Genesis through Deuteronomy) are the "history of the beginning of Israel and the giving of the Law of God." The books from Joshua through Esther are the "history of Israel." The rest of the Old Testament contains poetic and prophetic books that fit into various chapters in the history of Israel.

The book of Psalms, for example, is made up of individual songs that were composed by a variety of authors who lived at different times. To understand many of the psalms, it's beneficial to understand the time and situation of the author. So studying when the author of a particular psalm lived during the historical books, such as 1 and 2 Kings and 1 and 2 Chronicles, will help us better understand what he wrote.

Experiencing God by His Names does the "figuring out" work for you. Each name is in the order it's used in the Bible because God revealed His character through His names in a progressive manner. He opened people's minds differently throughout biblical history. For instance, "angel of the LORD," referring to the preexistent Christ, is given in Genesis 16, while others, such as "Morning Star," referring to the glorified Christ as the sign of a new heaven and new earth, are revealed only in the book of Revelation. God waited thousands of years of human history to share those unique names in Revelation because they are meant to display the culmination of His grand plan for the ages.

Getting the Most out of This Book

As you read and think about each of God's names, you'll come to understand 140 aspects of His character that will, hopefully, open your mind and heart to His magnificently complex Person. Each name written in this book gives you opportunities to internalize its meaning and to trust God to work His revealed character into your life.

There are a few additional features in each devotion to make your reading more meaningful. At the beginning of each devotion—after the name is given and the verse cited—is a short FYI (For Your Information) feature with a bit more information about the occurrence of that name in the Bible. I think you'll find it useful. You may find it interesting to know what was happening historically that led up to God placing that specific name in that verse. You may also use it to consider what God was trying to convey to the person or nation He was addressing. Why did the person or people use that name? I hope you'll come up with answers that will help you draw strength from that name and aspect of God when you face similar situations.

I've always found it helpful to read the context of the verse (the paragraphs or chapter before and after the verse cited) to put myself into the mindset of the people or nation involved. Write down the verses that are meaningful to you so you can work on memorizing them. When you encounter challenges to your faith that relate to the name you just studied, you can trust God to act according to His name.

Also in the FYI sections you may find more verses to enhance your understanding of God's specific character. Look them up in your Bible or pursue them on a Bible app using smart technology. Become a biblical detective and follow the additional information. To do this, you may want to spend two or three days investigating all the leads you find to take some of the mystery out of God's names so you'll understand Him even more.

At the end of each devotion, there are two application points:

- *Question for the Day.* Think about your answer to the question and ponder what it means for you personally. Don't rush on to the next name or wander to another subject. Stop and question yourself. Mull over the question. Ask God to open your heart and mind to better understand how He wants to affect your life through that particular meaning of His name.

- *Prayer.* You'll have an opportunity to talk with God regarding the aspect of His name you just read about. The prayer at the end of each discussion addresses God using that specific name. This will help you focus on the Lord using the name that relates directly to the need you're concerned about.

Jesus made this huge promise: "I will do whatever you ask in my name, so that the Father may be glorified in the Son. You may ask me for anything in my name, and I will do it" (John 14:13-14). Ponder that promise for a moment. Let it sink into your mind. He promised to answer all our prayers *as long as we ask in His name.* With the knowledge gained from this book, you'll be able to pray using God's names that relate specifically to your situation. Your prayers will be more intimate and meaningful. When you pray, you can consider, *What is my need that I want answered, and what is His name that corresponds most to that need?*

For instance, if you feel anxious or nervous, you can pray to God as the Prince of Peace. As such, He will bring His peace into your heart and mind. When making a decision, you can ask the Chief Shepherd to lead you to the right choice and to protect you from obstacles. God loves to respond to people who believe He'll act according to His character. When He answers those prayers He is glorified because it shows that the praying person really does know, believe, and trust in our Lord and Savior, Jesus Christ. This is *dynamic faith*—growing in knowledge and confidence in God's trustworthiness to do what He says He will do. Hebrews 11:6 states it like this: "Without faith it is impossible to please God, because anyone who comes to him must believe that he exists and that he rewards those who earnestly seek him."

Experiencing God by His Names isn't just for personal study and the development of your faith. There are many Christians who need to know the beautiful mosaic of God's character. If your loved ones, friends, and coworkers understand more of the mystery about God's names, would their lives improve? Would they more easily witness God working through their faith and prayers if they knew more about Him and obeyed Him more consistently? Sure they would. For these reasons, I encourage you to share what you learn about God through His names. You can do it. Jesus said, "A good man brings good things out of the good stored up in his heart, and an evil man brings evil things out of the evil stored up in his heart. For the mouth speaks what the heart is full of" (Luke 6:45). You may even want to start a small group to study the mysteries of God's names. Here are some suggestions for such a group study.

1. Spend one week on each name. Ask participants to become biblical detectives to find out as much as they can about that name. You can assign a variety of similar names for people to research.

2. Text or tweet each other during the week about what you're discovering. Put your discoveries on social media for your

friends to read about. That will encourage them to learn more about God.

3. In your group time, discuss the discoveries each person has made during the week. Some may want to give short reports. Some people may have questions to ask that will generate good discussions.

4. Invite the participants to share their needs and concerns. Then lead the group to pray for those things using the names of God that relate to the requests.

5. Find songs to sing together that use the names of God you're studying. You can even make up songs and poems about His beautiful attributes. Worship the Lord by praising His names specifically and thanking Him for how He's demonstrating His character in each person's life.

Finally, don't stop with the names explored in this book. Use them as a launching pad for further study and discovery about our wonderful Lord. In my other book, *Knowing God by His Names*, you'll find 206 names for God, along with lots of application ideas to expand your faith and trust Him to work in your life.

I'm convinced that the more you learn about God and His many names, the more you'll love Him. And the more you love Him, the more you'll trust Him to work in your life.

Angel of the LORD
Look Who Takes the First Step

The angel of the LORD found Hagar near a
spring in the desert (Genesis 16:7).

FYI: The term "angel of the LORD" (*Yahweh*) appears 54 times in the Old Testament. Ten of those times are in the book of Numbers. Most often, the name is a reference to God in human form—namely the preincarnate Christ. The angel of the LORD stepped into human history long before He came to earth as a baby.

God isn't sitting in heaven hoping we'll seek Him. If He was, no one would ever come to know the true God. All of us have sinned and gone our own way. Thankfully, however, *God steps in and intervenes* on our behalf. For instance, one time the angel of the LORD entered into a mother's desperate situation as she frantically ran away from a horrible situation.

Sarai was infertile and urged her husband, Abram, to father a child with her Egyptian slave, Hagar. But when Hagar became pregnant, Sarai mistreated Hagar so much that the slave ran away. She was an abused, pregnant woman with no food, no shelter, no particular destination—totally without help or hope.

That's when the angel of the LORD appeared to Hagar and told her to return to her mistress. The angel also said, "I will increase your descendants," and told Hagar about her future son. The angel of LORD initiated contact to encourage Hagar and save her life.

Have you ever felt like Hagar? Like no one cared, and you wouldn't be missed if you were gone? There is someone who cares about you—God! He will rescue you in your times of need. Call on Him now if you're in need.

Question for Today: Do you need to be rescued from something in your life? Do you need the angel of the LORD to intervene and give you hope? Ask Him.

Prayer: Angel of the LORD, help me keep my feet on Your solid ground instead of running away. Rescue me from the messes in my life and give me hope.

God Who Sees
No Darkness Is Too Dark

[Hagar] gave this name to the LORD who spoke to
her: "You are the God who sees me," for she said, "I have
now seen the One who sees me" (Genesis 16:13).

FYI: This is the only time "God Who Sees" (*El Roi*) appears in the Bible. The name *El Roi* is a combination of two significant Hebrew words. *El* means all-powerful, all mighty. It is the root of *Elohim*, which is translated "God," the first name given for our wonderful Lord in Genesis 1:1. *Roi* means "to see." When these two words are put together, *El Roi* means "the all-powerful God who sees everything in the universe."

The LORD God promised Abram and his wife, Sarai, that they would have a child even though they were very old (Genesis 15; 17:15-16). God told Abram that he would become the father of a great number of people. But after years of trying to conceive, Sarai couldn't get pregnant. She became impatient and told Abram to father a child with Hagar, her servant.

When Hagar became pregnant, Sarai treated her with jealousy and hatred. Hagar couldn't stand Sarai's abuse any longer, so she ran away into the desert. But Hagar couldn't escape *El Roi*, "the God who sees." God saw her in that dry wasteland where, perhaps, Hagar had thought no one would be able to find her. God saw her and came to her in her distress.

Do you think God sees you? Do you think He cares about you? When you walk in darkness or experience a time of distress, you may feel abandoned, lonely, powerless, or wounded. During those times, do you ask, "Where is God?" Perhaps intellectually you know that God is there, but emotionally you may feel He's hiding from you. Wherever you are, *El Roi* sees you. Even if you go to the most remote part of His universe, He still sees you. You may be surrounded by darkness, but He sees you as if you were flooded with sunshine. When there are no lights, it is difficult or impossible to see. You feel invisible to others in the darkness. But you are not invisible to *El Roi*! He sees you. You can be in the middle of a crowd of people and feel as if you're all alone…yet He sees you. When you feel abandoned, irrelevant, or lost…He sees. Hagar could not outrun *El Roi's* presence. Neither can you. When you feel you can't take one more step, He is there with you. You are *never* out of His sight.

Question for Today: When do you feel like God doesn't see you?

Prayer: God who sees, thank You for being here with me right now. Thank You for truly *seeing* me.

God Almighty
Power to Fulfill Promises

When Abram was ninety-nine years old, the LORD appeared to him and said, "I am God Almighty; walk before me faithfully and be blameless" (Genesis 17:1).

FYI: "God Almighty" in the Old Testament is a translation of two Hebrew words: *El* and *Shaddai*. *El* means "all-powerful." *Shaddai* means "breast." When these two words are combined, they mean "He is the all-powerful One who satisfies, nourishes, and sustains us."

Abram had a hard time believing that the Lord would give him a son in his old age. He was 99 years old, and Sarai, his wife, was 90. God spoke to Abram and said He would give Sarai and him a son even though both were well beyond child-bearing ages. *El Shaddai* brought life to their old bodies, and Sarai became the mother of Isaac (Genesis 17:15-16,19; 20:1-3).

Discouragement and disappointment are twins of the same parents—difficult circumstances and adversity. Expectations about life can be dashed when contrary circumstances hit. When you face times like these, you don't want to hear pious platitudes. You need real solutions. At such times, *God Almighty* shows up on your scene. He is the ultimate life-changer. What He promises, He will fulfill.

When you focus on yourself, you'll experience disappointments and weaknesses. But God hasn't left you alone! He is *El Shaddai*, the God who sustains and nourishes you—not by your strength, but by *His* life-giving strength. He is utterly faithful in all His ways. Because He is *El Shaddai*, He is worthy of your complete trust.

Question for Today: What makes you feel discouraged?

Prayer: God Almighty, bring me new life to defeat my weariness and discouragement. Do great things in me. Be *El Shaddai* in my life.

Judge of All the Earth
There Is Right and Wrong

[Abraham said to the Lord,] "Far be it from you to do such a thing—to kill the righteous with the wicked, treating the righteous and the wicked alike. Far be it from you! Will not the Judge of all the earth do right?" (Genesis 18:25).

FYI: "Judge of all the earth" appears only in Genesis 18:25. Sodom and Gomorrah were cities in southern Palestine near the Dead Sea. They were prosperous, important cities, but the people who lived in them were corrupt and evil. The Lord told Abraham that He was going to destroy the cities and their inhabitants. Abraham pleaded with the Lord to spare the cities if righteous people lived there. The Lord couldn't find ten innocent people.

Every day in the news we read stories about people who have victimized the innocent. History is filled with murders, frauds, thefts, scandals, and a host of other evil actions. Sometimes the judges who were supposed to uphold truth and justice were also corrupt. Wicked people go unpunished because of technicalities and bribes. Where is justice in those situations?

With God as "Judge of all the earth," we find true justice. He can only do what is right and just. And someday each of us will stand before this Judge of all the earth who knows our every thought, attitude, motive, and action. Evil and sin can't escape His knowledge or His judgment. No one can deceive Him or avoid notice.

Have you suffered injustice? Has a loved one of yours been victimized? Be assured of this: Someday all wrongs will receive just penalties, and the righteous will be vindicated by the Judge of all the earth.

Question for Today: How do you feel about the Judge of all the earth judging everyone? How do you feel about Him judging you?

Prayer: Thank You, Judge of all the earth, that You are just and can only do right.

LORD Will Provide
The Only Real Solution

Abraham called that place The LORD Will Provide.
And to this day it is said, "On the mountain of the
LORD it will be provided" (Genesis 22:14).

FYI: This is the only time *Jehovah-Jireh*, "Lord will provide," appears.

Abraham was rich, powerful, and loved the Lord. God had done the impossible—given Abraham and his wife, Sarah, a biological son in their old age. When Isaac was a teenager, God told Abraham to sacrifice him (Genesis 22:2). Abraham dutifully prepared to kill Isaac, but the Lord stepped in and provided a ram instead.

How do you think Abraham felt about the situation? How do you think Isaac felt? If you've been in a difficult situation, you can understand how Abraham felt that day on the mountain. Perhaps, like him, you were doing what God told you to do, but it somehow backfired. Who did you turn to for help?

Abraham obeyed God even to the point of being willing to sacrifice his only son, Isaac. God provided a solution that was beyond Abraham's expectations. When we follow God's commands in Scripture, He gives us the power and solutions to fulfill His directions. Will you trust the "LORD Who Provides" to supply His power to do His will and give you solutions when you face difficult situations?

Question for Today: In what areas of your life do you need the Lord's wisdom and solutions right now?

Prayer: Oh, *Jehovah-Jireh*, provide a solution for my situation today.

Fear of Isaac
A Healthy Kind of Fear

[Jacob said to Laban,] "If the God of my father, the God of Abraham and the Fear of Isaac, had not been with me, you would surely have sent me away empty-handed. But God has seen my hardship and the toil of my hands, and last night he rebuked you" (Genesis 31:42).

FYI: This reference to the "Fear of Isaac" is the only time this name appears (though a similar name is used in Genesis 31:53: "Fear of his father Isaac").

Fear is a reaction to something or someone that threatens us. We want to run away, hide, and avoid the situation. But there is another kind of fear that actually attracts us. It's a *good* fear that can be described as "a deep awe of God and His greatness." It's the realization of our frailty and of God's majesty and power.

According to Genesis 31, Laban couldn't find his household gods and accused Jacob of taking them. In responding, Jacob recounted the 20 years of hard labor he'd experienced working for his father-in-law (Laban). In his explanation, Jacob showed how he had been honest, hardworking, and faithful because he trusted the God of his grandfather Abraham and the Fear of Isaac (Isaac was Jacob's father).

The object of Isaac's fear was the awesome God who is far beyond finite human beings. He is infinitely wise and dependable. Isaac came to fear and reverence the Lord God, Creator of the universe, and the unseen God that his father, Abraham, trusted and obeyed.

The Lord God is not like the false gods other people follow after—power, fortune, sex, and success. These are attractive but ultimately empty. Seeking the one true God opens our hearts to trust in His righteousness.

Question for Today: Do you have a reverential fear of God?

Prayer: Fear of Isaac, You are so awesome, powerful, and majestic that I can't help but bow in fear and adoration. You, O Lord, are my God.

God of Abraham
The Past Affects You Now

"I am the God of your father, the God of Abraham, the God of Isaac and the God of Jacob." At this, Moses hid his face, because he was afraid to look at God (Exodus 3:6).

FYI: Moses was an 80-year-old desert shepherd when God spoke to him through a burning bush and told him to return to Egypt, where Moses had grown up. He was to lead the Hebrews out of slavery. Naturally, Moses had doubts. God told him to think back to the days of Abraham, Isaac, and Jacob. They'd trusted and obeyed their great God. Now God was telling Moses, "Well, I am that God! I haven't changed in all these years. Now, do like they did—trust and obey Me!"

Many people don't like to study history. They say, "I don't care what happened centuries ago." But the past can affect our present. It tells us how we got to the place we are right now. By looking at what people in the past did in situations similar to ours, we can learn how to respond.

We too can benefit by thinking back to Abraham, Isaac, and Jacob. Going back 3,500 years or so to Abraham's time brings to mind the kind of God Abraham followed and worshipped. Why did Abraham (Abram) leave everything he knew and loved in ancient Ur to head out to parts unknown? To find the answer, we need to look closely at his God (see Genesis 12). What was He like? What did He say, promise, and do for Abraham? How did Abraham respond? How could Abraham take his only son to the mountain to sacrifice him in obedience to God? (See Genesis 22.) Abraham so trusted God that he believed if Isaac died, God would resurrect him (Hebrews 11:19). Like Moses we can learn from Abraham and follow God as he did.

Question for Today: Who in history is an example to you for trusting God?

Prayer: God of Abraham, You are still the same today as You were then. You fulfill all Your promises. I worship You as my God.

I Am
Struggling with the Impossible

God said to Moses, "I AM WHO I AM. This is what you are to say to the Israelites: 'I AM has sent me to you'" (Exodus 3:14).

FYI: When we see "LORD" in the Bible, it's a translation of the Hebrew word *Yahweh* ("I AM"). Since the Jews didn't want to say *Yahweh*, they substituted the name *Jehovah*. It appears 6,823 times in the Old Testament. There is a different Hebrew name for God that has also been translated with the English word "Lord." To differentiate the two names, *Adonai* is translated as "Lord" using upper- and lowercase letters (see Psalm 110:1). In the New Testament, which was written in Greek, there is only one word, *kurios*, that is translated as "Lord."

Have you ever felt like God was asking you to do something humanly impossible? Maybe you've felt Him urge you to share your faith with a belligerent relative, boss, or neighbor. Maybe you felt a warning to leave your friends when they wanted to do something immoral or deceitful.

Sometimes God asks us to do things outside our comfort zones. "Nobody else is doing it," we say. "Why ask me?" How can we obey when every ounce of our being is screaming, "This is too difficult"? Instead of looking at our situation, the impossible request, or our inadequacies, we need to look at Who is asking us.

Moses listened to the Lord but hesitated to obey His audacious command to emancipate a million Hebrews from Egypt, the greatest kingdom on earth at the time. What could an eighty-year-old desert shepherd do to convince a tyrannical, despotic Egyptian pharaoh to let his slaves go?

But it was *Jehovah*, the I AM, who was sending Moses. The I AM wasn't one of the weakling gods the Egyptians worshipped. He made the universe and everyone in it. He set up and took down kingdoms. The I AM is always in the present. Time is His invention. Every second of human history is in the present tense to Him. When you obey Him, the I AM is always with you, giving you His powerful resources to do what He's commanded.

Question for Today: Is *Jehovah* asking you to do something hard? Will you do it?

Prayer: Oh great and awesome I AM, forgive me for giving excuses for not obeying You. I want to follow Your Word with faith and enthusiasm. I trust You for the strength to do even the hardest things.

God of the Hebrews
Leading Losers

*[God said to Moses,] "The elders of Israel will listen to you.
Then you and the elders are to go to the king of Egypt and
say to him, 'The LORD, the God of the Hebrews, has met
with us. Let us take a three-day journey into the wilderness
to offer sacrifices to the LORD our God'" (Exodus 3:18).*

FYI: This is the first time the name "God of the Hebrews" appears. The name appears five more times in the Bible—always in Exodus. Moses was told to go back to Egypt and lead God's people out of slavery. But to where? Egyptians lived in Egypt, but the Hebrew slaves had nowhere to call home. Egypt was a hostile land to them—no freedom, no property ownership, no hope. They were oppressed and depressed. Pharaoh laughed at and ridiculed the God of the Hebrews as a weakling and God of slaves. But the God of the Hebrews showed Pharaoh who was greater.

People like to be friends with famous people and powerful leaders. If we see someone famous, we want to get close and try to get an autograph. We wear T-shirts with our favorite heroes' names on them. Some individuals try to look like them or imitate them. Celebrity endorsements are a big image-builder in the marketing of products. We don't want to associate with losers. Instead we avoid or ostracize them.

God loves *all* people, even those the world puts down as losers or rejects. He associates with outcasts and slaves, the ones some people consider the lowest of the low. When we look down on people who are different than ourselves, we're showing a haughty spirit. The other people may look different, smell different, act different, think different, and even irritate us with their difference. God identifies with those who trust Him and follow His leading regardless of their stations in life. As the Egyptian pharaoh found out, whoever follows the God of the Hebrews becomes strong. God leads even the oppressed to become winners in His sight. God plus one person becomes a majority.

Question for Today: Do you call some people losers? Are they really? Are you willing to be thought less of by people as long as you have God's approval?

Prayer: Thank You, God of the Hebrews, for leading slaves out of bondage and empowering them with Your strength. You are my God, and I follow You.

Lord Who Heals
When Life Isn't Fun

[The Lord said,] "If you listen carefully to the Lord your God and do what is right in his eyes, if you pay attention to his commands and keep all his decrees, I will not bring on you any of the diseases I brought on the Egyptians, for I am the Lord, who heals you" (Exodus 15:26).

FYI: The name *Jehovah-Rophe*, "Lord Who Heals," appears only this one time in the Bible. After the Lord miraculously brought the Israelites through the Red Sea, they walked three days in the desert without water. Tired, thirsty, nerves on edge, they weren't trusting in *Jehovah-Rophe* to solve their problems. Instead they complained bitterly against Moses and God. Graciously the Lord told Moses to throw a desert tree into nearby polluted water to give them clean water. But God also warned the Israelites to obey Him to avoid future negative fallout.

Every day we read about tragedies in our world. We see the results of violent crimes in our neighborhoods, natural disasters across our plains, and wars in other countries. With the pain and suffering of our world so real and tangible, it's sometimes difficult to understand where God is in the midst of the turmoil.

But then we hear the stories about people who were rescued from horrible circumstances—earthquakes, floods, fires, and personal tragedies—and our faith is renewed, our hope is restored. Our journeys of healing begin when *Jehovah-Rophe* steps in.

The Lord your God wants you to choose to follow His ways regardless of the pressures that circumstances or people place on you. He basically said, "If you listen...if you do right...if you obey, then you will not face the consequences that others who disobey will face" (Exodus 15:26).

Every decision we make has consequences, whether we think so or not. Determine to make the kind of choices that have *good* consequences. Trust *Jehovah-Rophe* to heal you of the consequences brought about by your disobedience or the disobedience of others that affect you.

Question for Today: What temptation or decision are you facing right now for which you need healing? What circumstances are facing you where you need to choose the Lord's way?

Prayer: *Jehovah-Rophe*, please heal the areas of my life that are hurting. Let me know You are here for me, and You are healing me.

Lord Is My Banner
Who Fights Your Battles?

Moses built an altar and called it
The Lord is my Banner (Exodus 17:15).

FYI: This is the only time the name *Jehovah-Nissi*, "Lord is my Banner," occurs in the Bible. A banner, or standard, was the flag of a tribe, country, or king that an army fought for. It rallied the troops to fight as a united force. The powerful Amalekites had attacked the Hebrews as they camped in the desert after being freed from Egyptian slavery. The former slaves and brick makers were hard-pressed to fight such an experienced, organized army. But Moses prayed during the fierce battle, and *Jehovah-Nissi* gave them a great victory over a superior force. Moses built an altar as a reminder of the triumph the Lord gave to His people that day.

We all have battles. For one person it might be a battle to overcome an addiction. For another, trash-talking is a problem. Or it might be struggling with a volatile temper. Or maybe it's simply yielding to the same temptation time and time again.

The key to victory is not the power of the enemy, but, rather, the Source of your strength. The banner of the Lord is your rallying flag. As long as Moses held up his arms and prayed, the Hebrews were winning. When his arms came down, they started losing. As long as he prayed, the power of the Lord gave the Hebrew fighters courage and strength.

Like Moses, you can tap into the power of the Lord to conquer the enemies you're battling. Victory may not be immediate, but it is ultimately assured when you draw on the Lord and His resources.

Question for Today: What is your biggest enemy? Have you tried to find victory without success? Were you fighting in your own strength?

Prayer: Lord, You are the banner over me. You are my *Jehovah-Nissi*. Rally me to Your cause and strengthen me to be victorious.

Jealous
To Whom Are You Loyal?

Do not worship any other god, for the LORD, whose
name is Jealous, is a jealous God (Exodus 34:14).

FYI: This is the only time God uses His name "Jealous." The Lord gave us the Ten Commandments. The first two say, "You shall have no other gods before me" and "You shall not make for yourself an image in the form of anything in heaven above or on the earth beneath or in the waters below. You shall not bow down to them or worship them; for I, the LORD your God, am a jealous God" (Exodus 20:3-5).

The Hebrews didn't obey those commands. Even while Moses was receiving the commandments from God, the people were demanding that Aaron, Moses' brother and God's spokesman, make an idol for them to worship. He complied and fashioned a golden calf for them (Exodus 32).

The usual way we use the word "jealous" refers to someone who is envious and/or suspicious of another person. What comes to mind is a love triangle, where one is resentful toward a rival who is trying to steal a boyfriend or girlfriend. Human jealousy can lead to hatred and violence, but God has something different in mind when He uses the name "Jealous."

When the Lord uses "Jealous" about Himself, He isn't envious of some rival. No one can come close to usurping His throne, although many have tried. Another definition of "jealous" refers to guarding our rights. Because no one or no thing can compare to Him, the Lord exhibits a holy zeal to be the sole object of our worship. The Lord is a jealous God—that is, His *zeal* is enflamed that we worship Him only. He requires exclusive loyalty.

The gods of the modern world aren't made of wood, precious stones, or silver and gold. No, they are the attractions of the world that captivate our hearts and pull us away from the Lord. These idols are deceitful, leading followers to ruin and ultimate destruction. The one true God wants our allegiance to be exclusively focused on Him. The benefits of such zeal for Him are marvelous.

Question for Today: How loyal are you to God?

Prayer: "Jealous"—that's a name I wouldn't ordinarily call You, Lord. But now I know that You want my commitment to be exclusively toward You. Lord, I freely give You my undivided loyalty.

God of Gods
Your God Is Too Small

The LORD your God is God of gods and Lord of lords,
the great God, mighty and awesome, who shows no
partiality and accepts no bribes (Deuteronomy 10:17).

FYI: "God of gods" also appears in Psalm 136:2; Daniel 2:47; 11:36. The competing gods are idols and religions that are zeros compared to the Lord our God. Moses told the Israelites that their God had demonstrated that His awesome qualities were far superior in every way to the false gods of the nations surrounding them.

There is constant competition for our attention and allegiance. World religions, high-profile religious leaders, sects, philosophies, and ideologies clamor for us to follow them. Materialism, secularism, atheism, and other "isms" entice us to their philosophies.

We must make the right—and best—choice of Whom to follow... Whom to worship. There are thousands of gods and inventions of mankind we could choose from, but the Lord our God is far above all of them. He is so much greater there really is no comparison to the little gods of this world. Not one of them comes close to His supernatural power, total faithfulness, eternal existence, absolute truthfulness, profound love, and the rest of His supreme qualities. We are safe in His hands.

Question for Today: What or Who has your loyalty? Has your loyalty been rewarded?

Prayer: Lord, You are the God of all gods! I give myself totally to You.

LORD Who Makes You Holy
Clean Inside and Out

Keep my decrees and follow them. I am the
LORD, who makes you holy (Leviticus 20:8).

FYI: *Jehovah-M'Kaddesh,* "LORD who makes you holy," is found only in this verse. God gives it to show that only He can make something holy. The Hebrews were starting to accept the idol worship of the surrounding nations. One detestable local god was Molech. People dedicated their children to Molech and then burned them as sacrifices. Some people went to mediums to seek advice from the dead. God commanded that people who do such things must be punished severely.

Have you participated in an activity you knew was wrong according to God's Word? It looked exciting and fun, but there was a small voice inside your head saying, "Don't do it!" But you did it anyway. We sometimes blur the line between right and wrong. TV, movies, books, magazines, and the world espouse activities and attitudes that oppose what the Lord has revealed through His Word. Today the idea of right and wrong seems foreign. "Truth" is viewed as an individual choice. The result is that we rationalize our behavior to make what we do okay. But God has a just standard of right and wrong. Since He is holy, only He can make us holy. Think of that. He can make us like Himself!

Question for Today: Do you want to become holy? Can you do it yourself? Why or why not?

Prayer: LORD who makes me holy, I don't want to be like the world. I want to be like You.

God of Jeshurun
Majesty in the Clouds

[About Asher, the LORD said,] "There is no one like the God of Jeshurun, who rides across the heavens to help you and on the clouds in his majesty" (Deuteronomy 33:26).

FYI: This is the only time "God of Jeshurun" is used. At the end of Moses' life, God gave a predictive blessing to each of the tribes of Israel. He gave this description of Himself—"the God of Jeshurun"— to Asher. The children of Israel needed to know that God was greater than all of the idols of the world.

What do you do when you feel down? You could be riding high and suddenly hit a snag. Down you go into a slump. Or maybe things have been tough for a long time. You feel depressed and have lost hope. The struggles seem endless; the dryness of your soul brings misery. There are a lot of temporary pick-me-ups, but where is the lasting solution? It's found in the God of Jeshurun! "Jeshurun" means "the beloved one." Who is Jeshurun? It's a poetic term for the people of Israel.

Believers in Jesus are also God's people. The God of Jeshurun rides on the clouds in His majesty—brilliant, alive, magnificent—to help us. When troubles and darkness invade our lives, we can picture Him swooping down to pick us up.

Question for Today: Can you imagine God riding the heavens in majesty? If so, are you smiling with joy?

Prayer: God of Jeshurun, the clouds in the sky remind me of Your greatness. Wow!

Lord of All the Earth
Look Who Is Ahead of You

*See, the ark of the covenant of the Lord of all the earth
will go into the Jordan ahead of you (Joshua 3:11).*

FYI: Lord (*Adonai*) of all the earth appears five times in the Old Testament, including twice in the third chapter of Joshua (see also Psalm 97:5).

The Hebrews were on the east side of the Jordan River, and the Promised Land was on the other side. They had to cross the river and fight for the land. These children of emancipated Egyptian slaves were faced with the biggest challenge of their lives. Twelve brave men trusted the Lord and carried the ark of the covenant (a large, wooden box with long poles attached to transport it) ahead of all the people.

"Just go for it!" That's the advice some people give to get you moving. But the real question is, "Why are you hesitating in the first place?" Maybe you're tired, lazy, confused, uncertain, or scared. Maybe you're challenged by circumstances or pressures that demand courage as they force you to do something you really don't want to do. Though you have to do something about the situation, being told to "just go for it" doesn't help.

Can God give you the courage to go beyond your natural inclinations? Yes! When you need courage to conquer your fears and hesitation—go for it…with the Lord of all the earth.

The ark of the covenant of the Lord of all the earth symbolized God's presence to the Hebrews. They'd been wandering for forty years, and now they were on the east side of the Jordan River, which was at flood stage. There was no bridge or way around the rushing, violent waters. They might all drown! On the west side were their enemies—giants and fortified cities. The Israelites might be defeated and die. But the Lord of all the earth was the difference maker. He promised to go before them through the raging river and powerfully into battle.

As soon as the priests who were carrying the ark of the covenant ahead of the Israelites got their feet wet, *Adonai* split open the river. The people walked across on dry ground! Nothing you face is greater than the power of *Adonai*, Lord of all the earth! He owns everything and is in charge of every situation. He is greater than your fears, your reluctance, and your frailties. Trust Him to go ahead of you and prepare your circumstances for your victory.

Question for Today: In what situation right now do you need the Lord of all the earth to go before you and prepare the way for victory?

Prayer: Lord of all the earth, I desperately need You to go ahead of me in this tough situation. I'll follow You into raging waters and tough battles because I know You will always stand by me. Give me the courage to "just go for it."

Commander of the LORD's Army
The Supreme General

The commander of the LORD's army replied, "Take
off your sandals, for the place where you are standing
is holy." And Joshua did so (Joshua 5:15).

FYI: Joshua followed the directions of the "commander of the LORD's army" when he fought against Jericho (Joshua 6–7), Ai (8:1-2), the five kings of the Amorites (10:7-10), and many other cities (10:28–12:24).

Have you ever developed plans at work to accomplish something, but then someone higher up changed them? There is a phrase for this: They "pulled rank" on you. To "pull rank" means that someone exerts his or her authority to make the people below them do what he or she wants. Having people pull rank happens all the time. It happened to Joshua.

Moses was dead, and Joshua was chosen to be the leader of the Israelites and to be the supreme military general designated to lead the invasion to conquer the Promised Land. One day Joshua saw a man in front of him holding a sword. When Joshua asked who he was and whether he was an enemy, the man said, "As commander of the army of the LORD I have now come" (Joshua 5:13-14). The sovereign Lord pulled rank on Joshua.

Joshua immediately fell facedown and asked, "What message does my Lord have for his servant?" He obeyed his Commander-in-chief and submitted to His holy authority. The conquest of the Promised Land was accomplished by the Israelites led by Joshua under the direct authority of the Commander of the LORD's army.

How does that relate to you today? If you're going to win your battles, you need to trust and allow the Commander to pull rank on you.

Question for Today: Are you submitting to your Commander's authority and plans—even when they contradict your plans and strategies?

Prayer: Commander of the LORD's army, I submit myself to Your authority. I will obey Your orders and fight with courage the battles I face.

Mighty One
What's in My Head and Heart?

The Mighty One, God, the Lord! The Mighty One,
God, the Lord! He knows! And let Israel know! If
this has been in rebellion or disobedience to the
Lord, do not spare us this day (Joshua 22:22).

FYI: "Mighty One" appears nine times, always referring to God's power and authority: Psalm 42:4; 50:1; Isaiah 10:34; 33:21; Matthew 26:64; Mark 14:62; Luke 1:49.

Usually we think of "mighty" as referring to physical strength. We might describe a football player as mighty. "Mighty" doesn't usually refer to insights or discernment. Yet God uses "mighty" that way to increase our understanding of Him.

Per Moses' promises to the people before they entered Palestine, Joshua gave sections of the Promised Land, divided by the River Jordan, to the tribes of Israel. The tribes of Reuben, Gad, and half of Manasseh were on the east side of the river. When they built their own altar to the Lord on their side, the other tribes thought they were going astray and confronted them (Joshua 22:1-20).

The two-and-a-half tribes denied the charge. They said the Mighty One knew their thoughts and motives were innocent. They'd built the altar as a witness that all the Israeli tribes and their descendants worshipped the one true God (Joshua 22:21-31).

The Mighty One is so powerful that He knows our thoughts and motives.

Question for Today: Are your thoughts and motives pleasing to the Mighty One?

Prayer: Mighty One, You know my head and heart. Purify my thoughts and motives.

Judge
The Final Reckoning

[Jephthah, through messengers, told the Ammonite king,] "I have not wronged you, but you are doing me wrong by waging war against me. Let the LORD, the Judge, decide the dispute this day between the Israelites and the Ammonites" (Judges 11:27).

FYI: The noun "judge" appears 81 times, but only 6 times does it refer to God. In Jephthah's time, Israel had no king. They were ruled by a series of judges, usually military heroes. But God was *the* Judge.

Has anyone seriously wronged you? Left you feeling victimized and maybe scarred for life? Has there ever been a time when you felt abandoned? Those are terrible feelings, aren't they? Sometimes in those situations, we may find ourselves resenting—even hating—those who did us wrong. There may be a desire for revenge. It seems natural to justify how the persons who wronged us should be punished. Our stomachs get tied into knots when we think about the injustices. It's even worse when we perceive that the perpetrators are getting off free.

The Israelites didn't pick this fight with the Ammonites. God's people had lived among the surrounding nations for 300 years. However, the Ammonites grew to fear the Israelites, so they gathered a great army together in order to destroy them. Jephthah, the leader of Israel, sent a message to the king of the Ammonites to ask him not to start a war. The king rejected Jephthah's request for peace. Terror, war, and death were forced on the nation. Jephthah appealed to the Lord, the Judge, and the Lord gave the Israelites a great victory (Judges 11:32-33).

However, sometimes God does it differently. The timing and method of His just judgments are His decisions. He might bring recompense soon or wait until the final judgment, when life as we know it is no more. Rest assured, God is the final Judge, and He will right all wrongs. Give Him your pain, and let Him do the judging (see Romans 12:17-21). It may seem that evil is triumphing over good, but there is a Judge who will make everything right someday.

Question for Today: How are you handling the pain and grief someone has caused you? Are you acting as the judge or are you content to let God be the Judge in the situation?

Prayer: Oh Lord, You are the final, just Judge. You'll make everything right in Your timing and in Your way. I place my anger and revengeful heart in Your hands. Give me the courage to forgive people and be at peace in You.

The Glory
Manipulating God

The Glory has departed from Israel, for the ark
of God has been captured (1 Samuel 4:22).

FYI: The "ark of the covenant" was also called the "ark," the "ark of God," the "ark of might," the "holy ark," and the "ark of the testimony." It was a rectangular wooden box overlaid inside and out with gold, measured 45 by 27 by 27 (in inches; 114 by 69 by 69 in centimeters). Stored inside were the Ten Commandments tablets, a bowl of manna, and Aaron's rod. On the top was a gold plate called the "mercy seat" or "atonement cover," with two cherubim at the ends facing each other, wings spread upward and over the lid (Exodus 25:10-22). During the wilderness journey, it was carried by two long poles inserted through rings attached to the corners. When the temple was built, the ark of the covenant resided in the "Holy of Holies." This was where God met with Israel's high priest once a year. This was the holiest place on earth at the time.

When valuable and precious possessions are stolen, we feel the sharp pain of our sudden loss. Besides anger and bewilderment as to how it happened, we desperately want to get our possessions back and deliver the thieves to justice. We may also experience a sense of violation. These feelings are greatly intensified when someone we love is suddenly taken from us through an accident, illness, or violence. The finality of death creates an indescribable void. All those feelings are amplified to a large degree when an entire nation experiences a colossal tragedy. The ark of God, which symbolized the glorious presence of God to the Israelites, was seized during a battle with their archenemies, the Philistines. The Israelites had grown cold toward the Lord, but they reasoned that taking the ark into battle would force God to give them victory. But they were defeated (1 Samuel 4:1-11).

In addition to the tragic loss of the ark, the high priest, Eli, and his two wicked sons died. Eli's daughter-in-law was giving birth to a son. She named him Ichabod (meaning "no glory"), saying, "The Glory has departed from Israel" (verse 21). Then she died. To the Israelites, God had been captured. They'd tried to use God like a lucky charm, but it didn't work. God is nobody's puppet.

Question for Today: Have you ever tried to get God to do what you wanted? Have you viewed Him as a genie or good-luck charm?

Prayer: God, what a fabulous name for you: The Glory. You *are* glorious; all glory resides in You. I worship You and adore You. If I've tried to manipulate You, show me my sin so I can ask for Your forgiveness.

Glory of Israel
The Only One Who Will Not Lie

*He who is the Glory of Israel does not lie or change
his mind; for he is not a human being, that he
should change his mind (1 Samuel 15:29).*

FYI: Samuel was the last judge of Israel because the elders of Israel
went to him and demanded to be like the surrounding nations who
were ruled by a king. The Lord told Samuel to listen to them because
"it is not you they have rejected, but they have rejected me as their
king" (1 Samuel 8:7).

A lie is a false statement made to cover up the truth. When people tell one
lie, they often have to tell another lie to cover up the first one. Then they
tell a third lie to cover up the second, and on it goes.

Another way of covering up is to call the lie a half-truth, hoping that
the true part will negate the part that was a lie. When caught in a lie,
people try to soften the impact by saying the lie wasn't really a "big" one.

Saul was chosen as the first king of the united Israel (1 Samuel 10). God
blessed him greatly and gave him strength to lead His people against their
enemies. But over the years Saul became proud and slowly hardened his
heart toward the Lord and Samuel, God's prophet.

When Saul sacrificed sheep to the Lord, an event only a priest was
allowed to do, he was called out on it. When asked what had happened,
Saul explained that he was under great stress and needed God to act
quickly to defeat his enemies. He blamed Samuel for arriving too late to
make the offering. As a consequence, God told Saul his kingdom wouldn't
last and another person would be anointed king (1 Samuel 13:5-14).

Years later, Saul disobeyed God's explicit command again. He didn't
fully carry out God's orders during a battle. When Samuel confronted
the king, Saul blamed his misconduct on his soldiers (1 Samuel 15:13-28).

The Lord is the Glory of Israel! He doesn't tell white lies, half-truths, or
any other type of lie. There is no deceit in Him! You can totally trust the
Glory of Israel to do exactly what He says He will do.

Question for Today: Are you hiding behind any lies, white lies, half-truths, or rationalizations?

Prayer: Glory of Israel, how grateful I am that You're not like me. You are the Source of all truth and are totally trustworthy. Forgive my lies. Make me clean so I can walk humbly with You.

The Name
Where the Name Resides

[David] and all his men went to Baalah in Judah to
bring up from there the ark of God, which is called by the
Name, the name of the LORD Almighty, who is enthroned
between the cherubim on the ark (2 Samuel 6:2).

FYI: After the powerful leader Joshua died, Israel had no human king for a long time. God had instituted a theocracy, which meant He was their king. If the people trusted Him and followed Him, the Lord would govern the nation. But the people followed after all sorts of gods and human leaders, and their obedience to the Lord grew faint.

Moving is no fun. It takes many hours of planning and preparation to make sure all our belongings are packed and get to the destination. It's really great if we have willing friends to help us pack up and move.

David had 30,000 able-bodied young men to help him move. What were they going to move? The Lord Almighty's residence! For 400 years the ark was in the Jewish tabernacle located in Shiloh. But unscrupulous leaders took it into battle against the Philistines thinking they could force God to help them conquer their enemy (1 Samuel 4:1-11). But Israel lost the battle, and the Philistines captured the ark. Later they gave it back to Israel, and it was eventually kept in the town of Kiriath Jearim (1 Samuel 6:10-21) for 20 years until David captured Jerusalem and wanted the ark to be moved to his city so he could give the ark of God a permanent home.

"The Name" represented the very presence of the Lord Almighty. The ark bore the symbol of God and signified His Being. This ornate chest wasn't holy itself, but *the presence of God made it holy*. Wherever the Lord chooses to place His Name becomes His and expresses His Being (1 Corinthians 6:11; 2 Thessalonians 1:12). Believers in Christ bear His Name and are His by possession. If you're His, you bear the Name!

Question for Today: How are you bearing the Name and expressing God's character to the people around you?

Prayer: Lord, You were so gracious and powerful for Your people, who carried Your Name in the ark. Thank You that Your presence is in my heart.

The Rock
Managing Change

The LORD lives! Praise be to my Rock! Exalted be my
God, the Rock, my Savior! (2 Samuel 22:47).

FYI: Twenty-one times in God's Word, "Rock" refers to the Lord—four times in 2 Samuel 22 alone. David sang the song of praise today's verse is drawn from at the end of many battles against his enemies, especially King Saul. Through all David's conflicts, personal tragedies, and near deaths, his Rock stood firm and protected him. The Lord our Rock never changes. You can depend on that.

Sometimes we just want to get away. Get away from the busyness of work. Get away from the stresses of home life. Get away from our heartache or grief. But we almost have to be forced to actually get away to be still, to be quiet, to rest in the God Who is our Rock.

When you run, where do you run? The best place to run is to the Lord. He is our daily getaway, our Rock, who provides safety, security, and strength. What are the characteristics of a rock? Solid, strong, heavy, and unaffected by the weather. The meaning behind God as "the Rock" carries the connotation of being powerful, unchangeable, and protective. Contrary to all other rocks, our divine Rock is alive! Alive and supremely strong and stable. The fickleness of circumstances and time may affect us, but they don't affect Him.

When everything all around us is changing, we need to remember that God is stronger than we are and unaffected by all that's happening. We can depend on Him and never lose our footing. He can handle what we can't, and He gladly will take our weaknesses and give us His strength and rest.

Run to the Rock! You will never be disappointed.

Question for Today: On the terrain of your life, where do you feel like your feet are slipping? Will you depend on your steady and strong Rock to keep you on solid ground?

Prayer: God, You are my Rock. I stand with You in faith today. Please make my steps sure as I walk through life.

Strength
Power to Transform

I love you, LORD, my strength (Psalm 18:1).

FYI: David faced terrors day and night. There were many battles with the mighty Philistines. When he was exhausted, David and his men were taunted by giants, relatives of Goliath (2 Samuel 21:15-22). During these times, David sang praises to God for strength.

Remember when you were a child and the bigger kids picked on you? Did you ever say to yourself, "If only I were stronger, I would fight them—and win"? As we go through life we encounter bullies—people who push us around, gloat at us, or make us afraid. They can be powerful personalities who dominate and disrespect us, someone at school or work who wields abusive authority over us, even an addictive habit that defeats us, or memories of past shame that plague us. How can we win against those stronger than us? *We remember that the Lord is our strength!* Though "strength" isn't technically a name of God, this attribute is so much a part of His character that we can rightfully say, "God is my strength."

The word "strength" has multiple meanings. It can be physical strength to defeat enemies or it can be emotional strength to stand up to humiliation or walk away from insults. Character strength enables us to withstand attempts to pull us down or tempt us to make immoral choices. Spiritual strength gives us courage to fight the attacks of Satan. All these different types of strengths are found ultimately in the Lord.

We know the Lord loves us because He's always ready to empower us to defeat our enemies. When we feel weak and that we might give in to temptation, we need to shout to the temptation, "I trust in the Lord, and He is stronger than you are!" When a bad habit or addiction attacks our weaknesses, we can call on the Lord. We can seek other Christians to bolster our courage to persevere. Psalm 18:30 says, "As for God, his way is perfect: The LORD's word is flawless; he shields all who take refuge in him."

Question for Today: When do you need the Lord's strength the most?

Prayer: Oh Lord, my Strength, help me become victorious over the things that make me feel so weak. Thank You for loving me even in my weakness.

Refuge
Sometimes Hiding Is Best

God is our refuge and strength, an ever-present help in trouble (Psalm 46:1).

FYI: "Refuge" appears only in the Old Testament. It's a descriptive title for God. Psalm 46 was written by the sons of Korah, probably for temple worship. This psalm inspired Martin Luther to write the great hymn "A Mighty Fortress Is Our God."

There is a time to stand up and fight, as well as a time to seek a place to hide. When a hurricane or tornado is approaching, we look for secure hiding places. When the huge storms of life come our way, where do we hide? We all face overwhelming blasts that rock us to the core. The death of a loved one, the loss of a job, or being rejected can drain us emotionally and lead to depression or dread. In these times, where can we hide?

We can flee to God! He is our refuge, our hiding place. He's always ready to welcome us. We needn't be ashamed of being afraid. He knows we need His protection. His answers don't always come the moment we run to Him and ask, but they do come.

Yes, there are times when we need to seek advice from Christian friends, godly counselors, and other sources of God's wisdom. God uses these means to help us. But *first* we need to take refuge in the Lover of our souls. No one loves us more than He does.

Question for Today: Where do you normally go for refuge from life's storms? Do you find protection there?

Prayer: God, You are my refuge. I know I can run to You when I feel threatened. Thank You.

Lord, the LORD Almighty
Dishonoring God and Others?

*Lord, the LORD Almighty, may those who hope in you not
be disgraced because of me; God of Israel, may those who
seek you not be put to shame because of me (Psalm 69:6).*

FYI: "Lord, the LORD Almighty" is a combination of three frequent
names for God: Lord (*Adonai*), the LORD (*Jehovah*), and Almighty (*Tsebaoth*). *Adonai-Jehovah-Tsebaoth* appears twenty times; thirteen of
those times are in the book of Isaiah. Almost all of the verses express
the judgment of our great God against sin and wickedness.

If you've ever let someone down, you've felt disappointment, shame, and
maybe even some insecurity. When people are counting on you, it's difficult when you fail them. Perhaps you felt something similar when you
first became a Christian. Do you remember feeling like you had to be
perfect so you wouldn't tarnish Christ's reputation? Did you think you
couldn't mess up for fear that people who didn't know Christ might run
away even faster?

Those are all normal feelings. Entering into a relationship with Christ
means that we must allow Him to transform our hearts. We're called to
turn away from sin and live our lives the way He wants us to. If we stumble
badly, how does that affect other people? David shared some of those fears,
worrying that God would be disgraced because of him. Do you struggle
with sinful actions? Do you occasionally say things you know aren't true
or that are unkind? Our actions and words do affect people. When we do
sinful things, like David did, a tremendous sense of guilt floods us. Worse
yet, non-Christians may say, "Look at those people—and they say they're
Christians."

God doesn't expect us to be perfect. We do sin; we will sin. But a humble attitude and sincere apologies are great testimonies to the grace and
forgiveness of our Lord, the LORD Almighty. He will hold us account-
able to how we lived. But when our hearts are right before God, we don't
need to worry about disgracing Him. He knows our hearts, and when we
make mistakes He will fill in the gaps with His grace. The Bible is filled

with sinful people who humbled themselves before God and received His great grace.

Question for Today: Where do you feel like you've affected people this week both positively and negatively?

Prayer: Lord, the LORD Almighty, I know I'm unable to live according to Your Word without Your help. Please fill in my gaps with Your grace so that I may honor You today and show others who You are.

Lord Our Maker
Made Special

Come, let us bow down in worship, let us kneel
before the Lord our Maker (Psalm 95:6).

FYI: This is the only time in the Bible that the name "Lord our Maker," *Jehovah-Hoseem*, is given. The word "Maker" referring to God appears seventeen more times, but only in the Old Testament.

Push the pause button on your life right now. Look around and notice the things around you that other people have made. That chair, this lamp, those clothes, that painting—all things we enjoy. "To make" means to "bring into being by forming, shaping, or altering material." From existing materials people fashion a plethora of items.

God is different because He existed before there was anything. When He created the universe, He did it without any existing materials. He created *ex nihilo*, that is, out of nothing. There was nothing and then, by His creativity, God spoke and the sun, moon, and stars appeared. "By the word of the Lord the heavens were made, their starry host by the breath of his mouth" (Psalm 33.6). We can't explain how He did it. But "by faith we understand that the universe was formed at God's command, so that what is seen was not made out of what was visible" (Hebrews 11:3).

Take note that God *did not* speak man into existence. Rather, God chose to make man from something. He scooped up dirt and made a man—a totally different process than what He'd done with the rest of the universe. Genesis 2:7 says, "Then the Lord God formed a man from the dust of the ground and breathed into his nostrils the breath of life, and the man became a living being."

Look at yourself in the mirror. You were made special—different from everything else in the universe. The Lord your Maker uniquely fashioned you. He is the great God far beyond what anybody can imagine. Look at His creation! Look at what He made! How marvelous and infinitely wise He is. Sing praises to Him with your whole heart. Get on your knees and worship your Maker.

Question for Today: Why do you worship the LORD your Maker? Why would anyone *not* worship Him?

Prayer: Lord, when I look at the heavens and earth that You created, my lips praise You. When I see how marvelous You made human beings, my heart is ecstatic. Oh, LORD my Maker, I gladly worship You!

Maker of Heaven and Earth
Help! I Need Help!

My help comes from the LORD, the Maker
of heaven and earth (Psalm 121:2).

FYI: "Maker of heaven and earth" is found five times in the Bible, but only in the book of Psalms. Psalm 121 is called "A song of ascents." Jerusalem is on the top of a hill, so no matter from what direction people came to the temple, they would go uphill. As they walked up—as they ascended—their songs of praise would lift up their souls and hearts toward God.

Have you thought about how you would have done things if you were the Creator? The tendency might be to have made everything so life would always go smoothly and satisfy every creature's wants and desires. You would have no pain or heartache. No one would suffer or experience disappointments. There would be no tragedies. But the fact is, you're *not* the Creator. You must face every day knowing you live in a broken world that, hard as you might try, you simply can never make everything go right.

Here is the good news: Your God is the Maker of heaven and earth, and He is a lot wiser than you are. His ways and thoughts are higher than yours. He has a plan for His creation—and a plan for you—no matter what difficulties you encounter. The Lord knows everything about His creation. As the partakers of the troubles and suffering on earth, we need help—and a lot of it. Some troubles are small, such as getting a headache at night. Some are big, such as getting downsized from a company. Some are colossal, such as a tornado hitting a house or the death of someone. Troubles come in all sorts of packages.

The Maker of heaven and earth isn't sitting up in heaven waiting for the troubles you're experiencing to pass by. No, "the LORD watches over you—the LORD is your shade at your right hand" (Psalm 121:5). He can send relatives, friends, or medical personnel to bring comfort. Government agencies or charitable organizations may come to your assistance. But the ultimate Source of help comes from your Maker. He knows everything about you, including your dire circumstances. He can make the most difficult things turn into good for you (Romans 8:28-29). Your Maker molds and shapes you through tough times to develop in you all He wants you to be. How wonderful to know that "the LORD will watch over your coming and going both now and forevermore" (Psalm 121:8).

Why not go to Him for help right now?

Question for Today: How have you seen the Maker of heaven and earth help you in the past?

Prayer: LORD, Maker of heaven and earth, You are an eye witness of all You created. Your solutions are exactly what I need. Help me now in what I'm facing. Give me the confidence to trust You more every day.

Good Spirit
Educated to Do the Best

Teach me to do your will, for you are my God; may your good Spirit lead me on level ground (Psalm 143:10).

FYI: The only other time "good Spirit" occurs in the Word is in Nehemiah 9:20. "Teach me" appears nineteen times in the Bible, but sixteen are in the book of Psalms, and all are directed toward the Lord.

Schools are designed to pass on knowledge from one educated person to those who want to learn. Not every student wants to learn, but those who do will receive an education that will, hopefully, improve their lives. Yet, some teachers aren't qualified to teach. Others may be passing on a destructive education. For that reason, the *source* of a student's knowledge is critically important. Is the teacher passing on truths that will make us better people? Or is the teacher educating us in the wrong things? Who is the greatest educator of truth? It's the "good Spirit," sent from God the Father. And what is the greatest thing we can learn? To do God's will. So what's the real question? Are we hungry to learn the truth—God's truth? Many Christians have chosen to run their own lives or to sit at the feet of false teachers. These are "Christian atheists" because, although they say they believe in Jesus, they live as if God doesn't exist.

The Holy Spirit is called the "good" Spirit. Jesus commented on the importance of the word "good": "Just then a man came up to Jesus and asked, 'Teacher, what good thing must I do to get eternal life?' 'Why do you ask me about what is good?' Jesus replied. 'There is only One who is good. If you want to enter life, keep the commandments'" (Matthew 19:16-17). God alone is good. The good Spirit leads us "on level ground." We can trust Him to teach us to do His will for living the best life now and for eternity.

Question for Today: Are you a "Christian atheist" or do you sit at the feet of the "good Spirit" to learn God's will and ways?

Prayer: Good Spirit, I want to know and do God's will. Please teach me.

Loving God
Mercy Always Precedes Judgment

He is my loving God and my fortress, my stronghold
and my deliverer, my shield, in whom I take refuge,
who subdues peoples under me (Psalm 144:2).

FYI: This is a very personal psalm from David. Saul had hunted David for years in order to kill him. David even had to live among the Philistines, Israel's archenemy, to hide from the king (1 Samuel 27:1-12).

Many people think that God is always portrayed as angry and hostile in the Old Testament. They point to the judgments and curses He gives as evidence that He is vengeful. In fact, it's been said, "The God of the Old Testament is a God of wrath; the God of the New Testament is a God of love." It's as if there are two different gods. But there is only one God, and He is not a chameleon who changes with evolving events. Who He is in Genesis is who He is Revelation. In all cases, God is faithful and trustworthy, though at different times He displays different aspects of His character.

David knew God's love very well. For years the Israelite was hounded by his enemies. Yet whether he was hiding from Saul or sitting on the throne of Israel, David knew God loved him. When his enemies got close to killing him, he knew the "loving God" was his stronghold to deliver him and protect him. God was David's refuge (defense) from all his enemies. He would keep David safe and give him the power (offense) to win battles.

This loving God displayed a major principle throughout the Old Testament. I call it "mercy always precedes judgment." When you read the judgments and curses God gave, look at what comes before them. For many years (sometimes hundreds of years) prior, God sent His prophets who often performed miracles to encourage the Israelites to turn back to Him. But they repeatedly refused. His judgment came only after His love was rejected. Even then He was and is consistently the God of love.

Question for Today: When have you experienced God's love?

Prayer: Oh loving God, I don't deserve Your love, but You've consistently shown me how much You care for me. I'm so grateful. Thank You.

King of Glory
Look Who's Coming!

Lift up your heads, you gates; be lifted up, you ancient doors, that the King of glory may come in (Psalm 24:7).

FYI: "King of glory" is found five times in the Bible—all of them in Psalm 24. This psalm focuses our attention on the greatness and majesty of our great Lord.

God established the earth, and He owns everything in it. Everything we see, He made—including us. God has a purpose for us while we're on Earth, but participating is our choice. He gives special privileges for those who seek Him and endeavor to live with "clean hands and a pure heart" (Psalm 24:4). Those who honestly seek Him will experience His coming as the King of glory when the ancient cities open their gates to welcome Him in. He enters in triumph as the King of all the earth.

Who is this mysterious King of glory? None other than the Lord Almighty! He is the all-conquering Victor, and we revel in His victories when we conquer selfishness and evil in our hearts through His power. The King of glory is holy and magnificent. He's worth whatever it takes for us to work with Him to clean up our hearts, attitudes, and actions. Seeing Him in person will be more spectacular than anything we can imagine.

Question for Today: Have you lifted up your head and heart to worship the King of glory?

Prayer: Lord, today I lift up myhands in worship and open the doors of my heart to you. Hallelujah, you are King of glory.

God of Glory
All Nature Speaks

The voice of the LORD is over the waters; the
God of glory thunders, the LORD thunders
over the mighty waters (Psalm 29:3).

FYI: The name "God of glory" is found only twice—in today's verse and in Acts 7:2. The phrase "voice of the LORD" occurs twelve times in the Bible, and seven of those times are in Psalm 29.

We can feel so small and helpless when a severe thunderstorm passes overhead. As the awesome lightning strikes and mighty claps of thunder sound closer, people desperately seek shelter from the blast.

A powerful storm can cause great damage and death. The awesome display of nature reveals how tiny and fragile we really are. Who can possibly harness the power of these nerve-wracking storms? The Lord made the storms, and He harnesses them. Look at the immense sky, the vast oceans, and a delicate rose. All His exquisite handiwork reveals His glorious nature. The God of glory is far greater than any storm on earth. His voice breaks the trees, strikes with flashes of lightning, and shakes the desert (Psalm 29:4-9). The Lord descended in a fire and caused an earthquake that shook the mountain (Exodus 19:18). Yes, all nature surely displays His glory.

Everything in the universe obeys Him, and He sustains all by the power of His word (Colossians 1:17; Hebrews 1:3). He sits enthroned above the mighty waters and the powerful storms. However, the God of glory often speaks in a low, soft voice in our minds and hearts (1 Kings 19:11-13). The Lord uses His Word to show us His ways, and He gives strength to those of us who trust Him. Praise the mighty God of glory!

Question for Today: When you're caught in a powerful storm, what do you think about? Do you ever sense God's power as you consider nature?

Prayer: Awesome God of glory, how mighty and powerful You are! You speak, and the whole universe obeys. Lord, speak Your purposes and desires into my life.

Living God
Thirsty for What Satisfies

My soul thirsts for God, for the living God. When
can I go and meet with God? (Psalm 42:2).

FYI: The Lord will satisfy all who thirst for Him (Psalm 107:9; Isaiah 44:3-5; 55:1; John 4:7-14; 7:37-38; Revelation 7:17; 21:6; 22:17).

Working hard makes us dehydrated and thirsty. We crave fluids. In fact, our bodies contain up to 70 percent water. A person can live four to six weeks without food, but, on average, a person can live only eight to fourteen days without water. When we intensely desire water, mild to severe cravings motivate us to find something to drink.

In a similar way, we are spiritually thirsty. Do you thirst for more of God? Does your soul yearn to experience more of living for Him? Does your deepest longing drive you to think about Him and pray to Him every day? Just as your body can't survive without water, so your soul can't live without the living water that only the Lord can give.

If your soul is shriveling, make a change. Seek the Lord. Each day choose to meet with the living God and joyfully spend quality time reading His Word and talking with Him. He wants to satisfy your thirst!

Question for Today: Are you thirsting for the living God? What are you doing to relieve that thirst?

Prayer: Living God, my soul is thirsty for You. My heart keeps wandering away, but I desperately want to know You better and love You more. Draw me closer each day.

Rock of Israel
Follow the Right Leader

The God of Israel spoke, the Rock of Israel said to me: "When one rules over people in righteousness, when he rules in the fear of God, he is like the light of morning at sunrise on a cloudless morning, like the brightness after rain that brings grass from the earth" (2 Samuel 23:3-4).

FYI: "Rock of Israel" appears first in Genesis 49:24, then in today's verse, and then in Isaiah 30:29. David had many enemies, including Saul, the first king of Israel. Several times David was almost killed. After many extremely difficult times and battles, David brought peace and security to Israel. He acknowledged that the Rock of Israel was his leader and the reason he accomplished such great victories.

In your life, there may be many people who exert authority over you. Your boss. Your parents. The president of your country. With so many different people and groups managing and governing people, sometimes it's difficult to discern who to follow and whose leadership style is best to emulate.

What makes a leader great, anyway? The words David spoke revealed what he'd learned about leadership—the kind of leadership that honors God. He said that when a person reveres God and makes decisions based on holy living and God's principles, that person "is like the light of morning at sunrise" and "the brightness after rain."

A leader who follows after God's own heart—like David did—brings newness, and life, and hope. David made plenty of mistakes—and big ones too. But he loved God. David humbly repented when he sinned. He didn't give up on living under the direction of the Rock of Israel.

Question for Today: What prevents you from effectively leading the people around you? What can you change to be more in line with God's leadership style, which brings newness, life, and hope?

Prayer: Rock of Israel, shape me into the leader You want me to be. Show me how to lead like You do. Be my Rock.

Holy One
A Different Kind of Fear

The fear of the LORD is the beginning of wisdom, and knowledge of the Holy One is understanding (Proverbs 9:10).

FYI: The phrase "fear of the LORD" appears twenty-one times, ten of those in the book of Proverbs. It's also found in 2 Chronicles 19:7,9; Psalm 19:9; 34:11; 111:10; Isaiah 11:2-3; 33:6; Acts 9:31. "Holy One" appears many times throughout the Bible.

Fear is an emotion everyone experiences. Our usual reaction is to avoid the danger or fight the threat. Fear can be overwhelming, even paralyzing. The fear of death that strikes every person sooner or later may generate panic. Specific situations can cause us severe anxiety. But there is a totally different kind of fear that brings amazingly positive results.

The "fear of the Lord" *produces wisdom* in us. When we fear God, we desire to draw closer to Him. Some people interpret this fear as reverence. It does lead to that, but it's much more. With the wisdom the fear of the Lord produces in us, we learn to make good choices that honor God. We discover how to avoid evil. We gain in our knowledge of the God, who is pure, righteous, and kind.

Question for Today: Do you fear God in the way that brings wisdom and understanding?

Prayer: Most wonderful holy One, help me to fear You as I should. Fill me with Your wisdom and understanding so that I might please You in all things.

God of Elijah
God Doesn't Make Clones

[Elisha] took the cloak that had fallen from Elijah and struck the water with it. "Where now is the LORD, the God of Elijah?" he asked. When he struck the water, it divided to the right and to the left, and he crossed over (2 Kings 2:14).

FYI: The only people mentioned in the Bible who didn't die physically are Enoch and Elijah (Genesis 5:24; 2 Kings 2:11-12: Hebrews 11:5). Malachi predicted that God would send him back to earth. Some people believed Jesus was Elijah, but He was not (Mark 8:27-28).

Some Christians have dynamic faith. Their prayers seem to get answered. Regardless of the difficulties that hit them, they trust God to provide the way through challenges. Whenever we're with them, they encourage and lift us up. Maybe you've thought, "I wish I had faith like that. It would be great to be that close to God and experience His working in my life."

It's normal for Christians to have that desire, but God works in each life uniquely. It's good to learn from friends, but it's better to learn from God. Elisha discovered that. The prophet Elijah trusted God through many difficulties, and the prophet even raised a boy from the dead (1 Kings 17:17-24). His faith was so strong that he challenged 400 priests of Baal to call on their god to burn a sacrifice that had no fire under it. They couldn't, so he called on the Lord to burn the sacrifice dedicated to Him. Fire came down and burned the sacrifice, wood, stones, soil, and water (1 Kings 18:22-38). Wow! That was the God of Elijah.

Elisha, Elijah's servant and a prophet of God, wanted to be like his boss. After Elijah died, Elisha received his cloak. Naturally, he wondered if he would have the same relationship with God that Elijah did. The answer was yes and no. "Yes" because the God of Elijah was definitely with him, but "no" because God would empower him differently than He did his mentor. Elisha would go on to raise a dead boy (2 Kings 4:17-35), heal a leper (2 Kings 5:1-14), defeat King Ben-Hadad of Aram (2 Kings 6:24–7:20), and accomplish many other great things—even more than Elijah.

Don't envy other peoples' faith. Develop your own unique, loving relationship with God. Let Him work through you in His unique way.

Question for Today: Are you envying the gifts of others or developing your own personal relationship with God, trusting Him for the gifts that are uniquely yours?

Prayer: God of Elijah, all those who trust You develop a unique, loving relationship with You. I desperately want that. Draw me closer to You. Give me the gifts You envision for me. I trust You because You are my God.

Branch of the LORD
Mercy Brings Great Benefits

*In that day the Branch of the LORD will be beautiful
and glorious, and the fruit of the land will be the pride
and glory of the survivors in Israel (Isaiah 4:2).*

FYI: This is the only time "Branch of the LORD" is used. Throughout Scripture, God displays what I call His rock-solid principal: "Mercy always precedes judgment."

In botany, a tree is viewed as a plant with a stem that holds up the branches and leaves. The trunk supports and gives life to the branches to produce healthy leaves and fruit. Isn't it thought-provoking to think of God as a tree with a Branch that bears fruit?

For more than 200 years the Northern Kingdom of Israel rebelled against God and filled the land with pagan customs and idols. The people oppressed each other and plundered the poor. Isaiah prophesied that the Lord would bring judgment on the nation.

Even in His judgment, God is infinitely merciful. After the awful day of the Lord, He promised restoration and blessing. The Branch of the LORD will come and make the desolate land beautiful and fruitful. Who is the Branch of the LORD? He is the Messiah, who will rule the earth and establish God's kingdom. What a glorious day that will be!

Question for Today: How has the Lord shown You His great mercy?

Prayer: Beautiful and glorious Branch of the LORD, Your grace and mercy are magnificent. While I'm in this sinful world, help me keep trusting and praising You.

Lord
Magnificent Master

In the year that King Uzziah died, I saw the
Lord, high and exalted, seated on a throne; and the
train of his robe filled the temple (Isaiah 6:1).

FYI: "Lord" in today's verse is *Adonai*, which means "Master" or "Owner" of the universe. King Uzziah built a great army and brought national peace to the Israelites. Unfortunately, in his later years he arrogantly violated God's sacred temple. As a result, the Lord gave him leprosy, and he died in disgrace (2 Chronicles 26:1-21).

A tragic event can be a wake-up call. You're going through your usual routine when suddenly something traumatic happens. You stop, think, and reflect on what life is all about. The tragedy becomes a teachable moment when God breaks through to your consciousness.

Isaiah experienced the glory of God in the midst of tragedy. King Uzziah had been a good and powerful king of the Southern Kingdom of Judah for years. He'd built a great army, ruled over his enemies, and brought glorious riches to his country. But then he stopped following God.

After this great king died, the power and glory of Judah declined. Around that time, Isaiah had a vision of the ultimate ruler—the Lord (*Adonai*). The treasures of our world are mere toothpicks compared to the riches and glory of the Lord. Regardless of tragedies and difficulties, the Lord still reigns. Worship Him.

Question for Today: Are your eyes on the Lord or are they on the troubles facing you?

Prayer: Magnificent Lord, I'm awestruck by Your love. I fall at Your feet to worship You.

Lord Almighty
A Future That Helps You Live Today

*Everyone will sit under their own vine and under their
own fig tree, and no one will make them afraid, for
the Lord Almighty has spoken (Micah 4:4).*

FYI: Micah lived in rural Israel. He was appalled at the corruption, idolatry, injustice, and decadence of the big cities in Israel and Judah. He denounced false religiosity toward God and called the people of God to be faithful. His contemporaries were Isaiah, Amos, and Hosea.

If you've been in a frightening situation, such as being the victim of a crime, then you may have experienced fear or terror. Maybe you've even wondered where God was in the midst of your terrifying situation. Being children of God doesn't mean we won't experience what the Bible calls "the terrors of the night" (Song of Songs 3:8). However, God promises to work through all of the hardship we experience in our fallen world. He'll comfort us and walk with us through our recovery. He'll use every bad experience for good. These are promises He makes to all His children.

"Lord Almighty" is a magnificent description of the conquering general of the massive armies of heaven. He promises a wonderful future for those who have committed their lives to Him. He's here to fight battles for His children. He'll lead and guide us through every tough trial and painful situation. He is the most powerful commander and the most trusted leader. He's God, and He leaves none of His followers behind. He won't always work in the way we expect or show up in the way we may want Him to, but *He will show up*! He is always more than powerful enough to overcome any adversity we face.

Even though we can't comprehend it now or envision the accomplishment, the Lord Almighty says that someday He will establish the mountain of the Lord. He will teach us His ways so we can walk in His paths (Micah 4:2). After He conquers all the nations, there will be no more war, terror, devastation, or hostility. The nations will beat their swords into plowshares and their spears into pruning hooks (verse 3). God promises that we will ultimately experience personal safety and enjoyment.

Do you think these are empty and impossible promises? No, of course not! The LORD Almighty is powerful and faithful to do what He says.

Question for Today: What do you worry about or fear today? Is your fear reasonable in light of your LORD Almighty, your *Jehovah-Tsebaoth*?

Prayer: LORD Almighty, I trust You to lead me through the battles of life. Help me trust instead of fear because You are my guide.

Prince of Peace
History's Most Amazing Baby

To us a child is born, to us a son is given, and
the government will be on his shoulders. And he
will be called Wonderful Counselor, Mighty God,
Everlasting Father, Prince of Peace (Isaiah 9:6).

FYI: Jesus promised us a peace different than the peace the world offers (John 14:27; 16:33). God's peace is so desirable that the word appears 265 times in the Bible.

Can you imagine the shock people experienced when they learned what Isaiah had predicted? His pronouncement was during a time of national darkness. The Northern Kingdom of Israel had long put the Lord out of their lives and set up idols throughout their country. For hundreds of years, God sent prophet after prophet to call them back to the true Lord, but they refused. Foreign nations rose against them but still they wouldn't go to Him for help and hope.

The Lord is so merciful and gracious. Israel was experiencing destruction by foreign armies, especially the dreaded Assyrians. In the midst of such doom and gloom, God gave them the promise through Isaiah that someday the picture would totally change. A baby would come into the world and bring peace. The Prince of Peace—Jesus—did come approximately 700 years later! Jesus offers us His peace in the midst of our turmoil.

Question for Today: Where in your life do you need the peace that only the Prince of Peace can give?

Prayer: Prince of Peace, teach me to trust You even when I'm going through trying times.

Branch
Life Can Come Out of Death

A shoot will come up from the stump of Jesse; from his roots a Branch will bear fruit (Isaiah 11:1).

FYI: The only other time the name "Branch" refers to the Messiah is Jeremiah 23:5. The Branch is "a King who will reign wisely and do what is just and right."

When a man with a chainsaw cuts down a tree, it usually dies. Although it's rare, sometimes there is still life in the stump and roots. Slowly, a new shoot grows right from the stump. This is a sign that life can come from what was thought to be dead.

In today's verse, was God talking about a cut-down tree reviving? No. This promise has nothing to do with a tree stump. Instead, it's all about a *family* tree. Jesse was the grandson of Boaz and Ruth and the father of King David, who was Israel's greatest king. God promised David, "Your house and your kingdom will endure forever before me; your throne will be established forever" (2 Samuel 7:16). From the "dead" stump of Jesse and the royal lineage of David will come the Branch, the Messiah, who will bring blessing to all who trust Him. From the resurrection of Jesus, life comes out of death.

Question for Today: Are you clinging to the Branch for life?

Prayer: Lord Jesus, You are the promised Branch, the promised Messiah. You have borne fruit throughout the generations, and You gave me life in You. I praise Your name!

Spirit of the LORD
Resources Beyond Your Imagination

*The Spirit of the LORD will rest on him—the Spirit of wisdom
and of understanding, the Spirit of counsel and of might, the
Spirit of the knowledge and fear of the LORD (Isaiah 11:2).*

FYI: Isaiah 11:1-9 is a messianic passage predicting what the coming Messiah would be like. Written approximately 700 years before Jesus came to earth, Isaiah describes what the Spirit of the LORD would do in and through the Messiah. The Bible says about Jesus, "The one whom God has sent speaks the words of God, for God gives the Spirit without limit" (John 3:34). God will give you the Holy Spirit without limit. Mentioned twenty times in the Old Testament, "the Spirit of the LORD" comes upon various people, providing great power, wisdom, and knowledge to do mighty things for God.

It's difficult to admit that we need help. We're supposed to be self-motivated and independent. When tough times come, we may put on brave faces, but inside we feel fearful, disheartened, and discouraged. Our air of independence is gone. Who or what can pick us up and give us insights into how to deal with our situation? We all go through dark times when we feel lost, confused, and want to give up. Where do we go when we're backed into a corner? A friend? A book? A bottle of alcohol? A pain pill? How about the invisible God who is over all things?

The Spirit of the LORD can do what no book, bottle, drug, or human being can. Friends can rally around us with encouraging words. A good book might give us some insights. But friends and books are limited in their understanding of our situation. They aren't enough and, besides, they can't be with us all the time to solve our problems. The Spirit of the LORD can, however!

If you've received Christ into your life, the Spirit of the LORD lives in you right now. He is also the Spirit of wisdom and of understanding to give you insights and knowledge of how to handle your most perplexing situations. Because He is also the Spirit of counsel, He will give you solutions and hope so you can find your way out of the darkness. He'll give you the strength to choose victory and move forward with confidence. He is the Spirit of might! As the Spirit of the knowledge and fear of the LORD, He'll open your mind to the full character of God. This way you can love Him with your whole being and trust Him for great things in your life. God is with you—not just when you have problems, but for every second of your life. Trust Him and follow His guidance.

Question for Today: Why do you need the Spirit of the LORD right now?

Prayer: Spirit of the LORD, help me right now. I want to be filled with You and experience all that You want to give me. Guide me to use the resources You provide so I can live victoriously.

Most High
Good Boasting

*I [Satan] will ascend above the tops of the clouds; I will
make myself like the Most High (Isaiah 14:14).*

FYI: According to Bible prophecy, Satan has devised his "anti-Trinity,"
which consists of the beast, the false prophet, and the devil himself
(Revelation 16:13-14). Someday God Almighty will defeat them and
cast them into the lake of fire that burns forever (Revelation 20:10).

Do you know people who boast about their accomplishments? In school
they gloated about their test scores or athletic successes. At work, they brag
about their achievements. They drop the names of important people they
know. These people put others down by raising themselves up. Sometimes
their boastings are subtle and manipulative, at other times they're obnox-
ious and arrogant—especially when their bragging is aimed at making us
feel inferior.

As hard as that is to tolerate, can you imagine hearing someone proclaim that he or she is as great as God? Isaiah describes something that likely
happened in heaven. The "morning star, son of the dawn" was cast down
to earth for rebelling against God (Isaiah 14:12). Today's verse describes
Satan's arrogant boasting, as does this: "I will ascend to the heavens; I will
raise my throne above the stars of God; I will sit enthroned on the mount
of assembly, on the utmost heights of Mount Zaphon" (verse 13).

Satan was originally the highest creation of God. But he decided he
wanted to be like the Most High. But that can never be. The Most High is
sovereign over everything and everybody in all creation, including heaven.
Nothing and no one can come close to usurping His authority. All chal-
lengers will be resolutely defeated, as was Satan and his followers.

As believers in Jesus Christ, our boast is in Him and that we've been forgiven through His sacrifice on the cross (Galatians 6:14; Philippians 3:3).

Question for Today: What are you boasting about today? Make sure it's
only about the forgiveness of your sins and your salvation through Jesus.

Prayer: Most High, Your throne is above all. I gladly boast that I am forgiven
of my sins and am saved through Your Son. I praise Your powerful name.

Rock Eternal
Stability When All Else Is Coming Apart

Trust in the LORD forever, for the LORD, the LORD
himself, is the Rock eternal (Isaiah 26:4).

FYI: This is the only time "Rock eternal" is given in the Bible. The phrase "the LORD, the LORD" is an unusual construction. The first LORD is *Jah*, an abbreviation of *Jehovah*. This magnificent phrase is found here and in Exodus 34:6 and Isaiah 12:2.

"As solid as a rock" is a simile comparing an object, statement, or person to the characteristics of rock—strong, stable, constant, and durable.

In 1775, Reverend Augustus Montague Toplady was walking outside when a fierce storm suddenly came upon him. In desperation, he hid in a large crack in a nearby boulder. While in this formidable shelter, he scribbled down lyrics on a playing card for what would become the famous hymn "Rock of Ages." The storm raged, but the reverend was safe in the cleft of the rock. Today's verse from Isaiah was the inspiration for the hymn.

In Isaiah's time, Moab bordered Israel to the southeast. The Moabites were constant troublemakers. The prophet predicted that the Moabites' fortified cities would crumble (Isaiah 25:10-12). Then the Israelites would see that the Lord was stronger than their archenemy. Therefore, the Lord's people were commanded to trust in God because He would never fail them.

No matter how strong the opposition, the Lord is more powerful than the present danger. He provides perfect peace and stability to those who trust Him. The pressures on you might seem overwhelming right now, but the Rock Eternal will give you the strength to make it through the storm. "To trust God" means to renounce all dependence on self and people and, instead, rely completely on the Lord.

Question for Today: Are you entrusting everything in your life to the Rock Eternal or are you holding something back?

Prayer: Rock Eternal, bring me Your strength to handle the temptations that badger me. Give me Your peace in the midst of my troubles. You are totally trustworthy forever. What a great God You are. You are my Rock!

Holy One of Jacob
The Wow Factor

When they see among them their children, the work
of my hands, they will keep my name holy; they will
acknowledge the holiness of the Holy One of Jacob, and
will stand in awe of the God of Israel (Isaiah 29:23).

FYI: This verse in Isaiah is the only place in the Bible this name is given. "Jacob" is a synonym for the nation of Judah.

The "wow factor" is something that goes way beyond people's expectations. Let's face it: Talk is cheap. Anyone can promise anything, but only the results can validate the truthfulness of the promise. The "wow" shows that the preparation and hard work paid off. God gives us lots of "wows" throughout the Bible.

One wow is when Isaiah prophesied against the wickedness of Jerusalem (*Ariel*). It was the beloved city of David where God said He'd dwell on earth (Psalm 135:21). For more than 200 years the Israelites filled the city with idolatry, injustice, and violence. God kept asking them to return to Him, but they refused. The Holy One of Jacob was offended by the constant rebellion, so judgment was coming. Yet in His great mercy, God promised the city would be restored to a peaceful place and gives the promise in today's verse. When the Israelites see the results, they'll return to worshipping the God of Israel.

Question for Today: When have you experienced a wow from the Holy One of Jacob?

Prayer: Holy One of Jacob, I'm in awe of You. Make me more like You each day.

Creator of the Ends of the Earth
Looking at Yourself

Do you not know? Have you not heard? The LORD
is the everlasting God, the Creator of the ends of
the earth. He will not grow tired or weary, and his
understanding no one can fathom (Isaiah 40:28).

FYI: The Bible has its share of complainers. Here's a short list of some people who groused: Abraham (Genesis 21:25), the Israelites (Exodus 15:24; Numbers 11:1), Job (Job 7:11), the Pharisees (Luke 5:30), the Jews (John 6:41), Jesus' disciples (John 6:61), followers of Christ (James 5:9; 1 Peter 4:9).

Complaining is so easy to do. As soon as something happens we don't like, we gripe and moan. Kids complain, "It's not fair!" when they don't get their way. As we grow older, we don't stop grumbling. We rationalize our whining, and then turn on God. "How come this is happening to me?" we ask. "I don't deserve this!" We think God has forgotten us.

Our complaining turns us from grateful followers of Christ to people with a "woe is me" attitude. When we find ourselves complaining, let's consider it a wake-up call. We can ask ourselves, "Do I really know who God is? Do I get that He is the Lord *Jehovah*, the I AM, who rules the universe?" Our God is the everlasting God, eternally all-powerful and ready to defeat any circumstance, bad person, or whatever is contrary to His will. And in case we've forgotten, He is also the Creator of the ends of the earth, which includes you and me. He hasn't forgotten us! We haven't faded out of His sight.

I encourage you to get your eyes off yourself and your circumstances. "Lift up your eyes and look to the heavens: Who created all these?" (Isaiah 40:26). If you really see God in all His wisdom and power, you'll look differently at your situation. "[The LORD] gives strength to the weary and increases the power of the weak" (verse 29). Your faith unleashes His resources into your life. Turn your complaining into trusting God.

Question for Today: When you focus on the Lord, how does that change your perceptions?

Prayer: Dear Creator of the ends of the earth, help me turn my eyes away from me and toward You. Your greatness and wisdom far surpass my measly circumstances. Strengthen me to focus on You and Your resources.

Holy One of Israel
Seeing Is Believing

[I, the LORD, will answer] so that people may see and know, may consider and understand, that the hand of the LORD has done this, that the Holy One of Israel has created it (Isaiah 41:20).

FYI: Even when a close friend tells you about marriage, it's difficult to imagine what it will be like. You'll understand so much more after the wedding.

People use various sayings to express doubt: "Seeing is believing," "The proof is in the pudding," and "Show me, and then I'll believe." Putting faith in God is sometimes difficult because we can't physically see Him. So where is the concrete evidence? God's actions give results only He can produce. He promised the rebellious Israelites that after difficult times there would be prosperity and peace. Rivers would flow on barren heights, the desert would be turned into pools of water, and junipers would grow in the wasteland (Isaiah 41:18-19). How will they believe God can do all that? When it happens.

If you research Israel today, you'll discover semiarid regions have become lush farmlands, Mount Tabor and Mount Meron get plenty of rainfall, and Upper Galilee thrives with orchards. We say, "Show us, and then we'll believe." God says, "Believe, and I will show you." Genuine faith is *trusting God to do what He says.*

Question for Today: Do you see the Lord working in your life? Do you glimpse His future for you?

Prayer: Holy One of Israel, creation reveals Your wisdom and power. I worship You.

Creator of the Heavens
The Expert on the Chosen One

This is what God the LORD says—the Creator of the heavens, who stretches them out, who spreads out the earth with all that springs from it, who gives breath to its people, and life to those who walk on it: "I, the LORD, have called you in righteousness" (Isaiah 42:5).

FYI: The Lord created the universe and everything in it (Psalm 89:11; 90:2; 146:6; Matthew 19:4).

An expert is someone who knows a subject better than most people. If you want to invest your money wisely, you choose an expert financial advisor to build your portfolio. If a doctor tells you surgery is needed, you want the best surgeon to operate on you. When an expert offers advice, you listen more intently than if a friend gives his or her opinion. Experts know more.

God is the greatest expert on the universe and everything in it—and the most trusted expert for all things. God revealed something so colossal that no other expert could possibly speak knowledgeably on it. What was this critical topic? The coming Messiah. Contrary to the beliefs of the Israelites that the coming Messiah would be a military hero, the Lord said that the Chosen One would bring justice, but He would "not shout or cry out, or raise his voice in the streets. A bruised reed he will not break, and a smoldering wick he will not snuff out" (Isaiah 42:1-3). How could the Messiah be like that?

The Creator of the heavens authoritatively states that someday the Coming One will arrive with a distinct mission to both Jews and Gentiles: "to open eyes that are blind, to free captives from prison and to release from the dungeon those who sit in darkness" (Isaiah 42:7). Who are you going to believe about Jesus and His purpose? A human expert giving his or her opinion or the Creator of the heavens?

God sent the Messiah to set you free. You can trust Him to free you from whatever is trying to overpower you.

Question for Today: What do you want the Creator of the heavens to do in your life today? From what would you like to be free?

Prayer: Creator of the heavens, You are so wise. You made everything beautiful and sent Your Chosen One to solve my sin problem. I can trust You in all things—and I do.

Israel's Creator
Finding the Origin

I am the LORD, your Holy One, Israel's
Creator, your King (Isaiah 43:15).

FYI: Isaiah prophesied around 700 BC. The time from Abraham to the final kings of Israel was approximately 1,300 years. Throughout those generations, most of the Israelites rejected the Lord as their Creator, but a faithful minority trusted and obeyed Him. Through the prophet Isaiah, a merciful God was calling the Israelites back to their original purpose.

Astronomers, astrophysicists, and cosmologists study celestial bodies and other phenomena throughout the universe. One of their interests centers on trying to understand how the universe came into existence. Other scientists conduct experiments to discover the origins of life on earth. Scholars investigate the origin of birds, human beings, language, political systems, continents, and countless other topics. How did time start? How did civilization begin? How did nations come into being? To know the origins helps answer so many questions about the present.

The Bible describes the beginning of many things, including the universe, earth, plants, animals, and human beings. Much of the Bible centers on the origin and development of one nation—Israel. The Israelites came from one source. Circa 2000 BC, the Lord led one man, Abram, along with his wife, from their home in Harran (in what today is southeastern Iraq) and established them in Canaan (Genesis 12:4-5). What was His purpose? To make a great nation from Abram's descendants, that "all peoples on earth will be blessed through you [Abram]" (Genesis 12:1-3). The Lord changed his name from Abram ("father") to Abraham ("father of nations") to proclaim that his descendants would fill the earth (Genesis 17:1-8).

Later God says, "You, Israel, my servant, Jacob, whom I have chosen, you descendants of Abraham my friend, I took you from the ends of the earth, from its farthest corners I called you. I said, 'You are my servant'; I have chosen you and have not rejected you" (Isaiah 41:8-9).

The Israelites were supposed to serve the Lord, their Creator, and to show the world what He was like so all the nations would come to know Him and choose to serve Him. But the Israelites failed to honor and glorify God. Their waywardness and unfaithfulness led God to bring judgment on them so the nation would come back to Him. He was their Redeemer, Creator, and King. When the people loved and glorified Him, they were fulfilling their original purpose.

Did you know God created you for the same purpose? To love and glorify Him?

Question for Today: How are you fulfilling your purpose on earth—to love and glorify God?

Prayer: Israel's Creator, You created Israel for the purpose of glorifying You. That is what I want to do with my life. Please glorify Yourself in and through me.

God of All the Earth
The Faithful Husband

Your Maker is your husband—the Lord Almighty is
his name—the Holy One of Israel is your Redeemer;
he is called the God of all the earth (Isaiah 54:5).

FYI: The Lord says He is Israel's husband (Jeremiah 3:14; 31:32; Hosea 2:16,19-20). Someday the church—all believers in Jesus Christ—will be His bride (Revelation 19:7; 21:2).

The bride is the center of attention at a wedding. When she gracefully walks down the aisle wearing her gorgeous wedding dress, everyone focuses on her. She smiles radiantly and fixes her gaze on her beloved. The atmosphere pulsates with joy, hope, and love.

But what if the bride was a fickle prostitute who had been unfaithful to her husband? And what if the husband was remarrying her? That wedding would certainly be different! All the guests would be wondering why the groom wanted to do this again. What did he see in her that no one else did?

The nation of Israel was like an unfaithful prostitute. The Lord Almighty had chosen Abram, from the city of Ur, to live in Canaan so He could build the great nation of Israel from the man's descendants. To seal His promise, God changed Abram's name to Abraham, which means "father of nations" (Genesis 17:5). For more than 1,300 years, from Abraham to Isaiah, the Holy One of Israel showed how deeply He loved His people. He lavished miraculous gifts on them. The nation was the Maker's precious beloved. He created her to be His lovely bride—His bride who would display His glory: "Your Maker is your husband—the Lord Almighty is his name" (Isaiah 54:5).

But, instead, Israel kept prostituting herself with godless nations and worshipping gods detestable to the Lord Almighty. Israel eventually depended on other nations for protection, rather than trusting in the God of all the earth. God created Israel to be His bride, but she continually rejected Him.

Time after time, the Redeemer brought Israel back to Himself, but she ran away again and again. In the midst of her fickleness and rebellion, the

God of all the earth continued to show His great heart. He punished Israel for the evil and idolatry she perpetrated over the many centuries, yet He still loved her. He promised to someday redeem her once and for all. Israel would someday return to her perfect Husband to dwell in peace and bear many children (Isaiah 54). At that wedding, instead of all focus being on the bride, everyone will be looking at the God of all the earth. He is her magnificent, faithful lover.

Question for Today: Are you fickle toward the One who loves you infinitely—the God of all the earth?

Prayer: What an amazing story of Your faithful love, God of all the earth. I'm often just like Israel—continually vacillating in my commitment to You. Please forgive me. Thank You for still loving me when I fail You. Help me to be more faithful.

Spirit of the Sovereign Lord
A Mission to Accomplish

*The Spirit of the Sovereign Lord is on me, because the Lord
has anointed me to proclaim good news to the poor. He has sent
me to bind up the brokenhearted, to proclaim freedom for the
captives and release from darkness for the prisoners (Isaiah 61:1).*

FYI: This is the only time "Spirit of the Sovereign Lord" occurs. However, "Sovereign Lord" by itself appears 293 times in the Old Testament. "Sovereign Lord" consists of two words: *Adonai* and *Jehovah*. Jesus said He was *Adonai* (Matthew 22:41-44; Mark 12:36, Luke 20:42; Acts 2:34). *Adonai* is "God the Son," *Jehovah* is "God the Father," Spirit is the "Holy Spirit." "Spirit of the Sovereign Lord" refers to the Trinity.

When believers in Jesus Christ go on mission trips, they're usually sent by their church or organization to do certain tasks. They may be helping a mission for inner-city people, an orphanage in another country, or giving help in other areas. Likewise, Jesus was commissioned with a critical task that we know as the gospel.

Around 700 years after Isaiah penned today's verse, Jesus was born on earth. After He passed thirty, He read today's passage in the synagogue and added, "Today this scripture is fulfilled in your hearing" (Luke 4:21). Jesus accomplished His mission.

Question for Today: Have you seen the good news proclaimed and people released from darkness?

Prayer: Spirit of the Sovereign Lord, help me continue Jesus' mission.

King of Israel
Best Form of Government

The LORD, the King of Israel, is with you; never again
will you fear any harm (Zephaniah 3:15).

FYI: The Lord Jesus is called "king of Israel" four times (Matthew 27:42; Mark 15:32; John 1:49; 12:13). These, along with the Zephaniah verse, are the last five times "king of Israel" is used in the Bible.

A monarchy is government where the power of the state is given to one person who generally rules for life. The monarch possesses authority over their entire kingdom. In ancient days, when monarchs died, their position and authority were usually passed on to their first male offspring.

The Lord, King of Israel, doesn't rule like a monarchy or like a democracy, where the people give the power to govern to elected officials. The phrase "king of Israel" appears 185 times in the Old Testament referring to human rulers, but the verse in Zephaniah is the only incidence where the title refers to God. He didn't inherit His position and authority, of course. Nor was He ever elected, like in a democracy. He wasn't a dictator who forcibly usurped a previous ruler's position. God ruled and rules as a theocracy. The Lord rules absolutely the entire universe. He answers to no one. In today's passage, He says He is the real King of Israel.

In the past, the Lord allowed other nations to conquer Israel and subjugate His people because of the Israelites' grievous sins. But the King of Israel will ultimately conquer all nations and free His people to serve and worship Him alone (Zephaniah 3:9-10). Then there will be great gladness and rejoicing (verses 14-15).

Question for Today: Are you the monarch of your life or are you governed by a theocracy?

Prayer: LORD, King of Israel, You are my King. You are the most powerful and gracious leader in the universe. I sing praises to You! I rejoice that I'm one of Your subjects in Your eternal kingdom.

King of the Nations
Are You Listening?

Who should not fear you, King of the nations? This is your due. Among all the wise leaders of the nations and in all their kingdoms, there is no one like you (Jeremiah 10:7).

FYI: This name appears only one other time in the Bible: Revelation 15:3. God is also called "King of all the earth" (Psalm 47:70), "King of glory" (Psalm 24:7), "King of heaven" (Daniel 4:37), "King of Israel" (John 1:49), "King of kings" (1 Timothy 6:15), and "king of the Jews" (Matthew 27:11).

One of the most important tasks for a speaker is to get the attention of his or her audience. To assume people want to hear the speaker isn't a good idea. Each individual in a crowd comes thinking about what concerns him or her—or perhaps some other distraction that pulls away their focus.

After Solomon died in 931 BC, Israel had a civil war and split into two nations. The northern ten tribes were called "Israel." The southern two tribes were called "Judah."

The Southern Kingdom of Judah had a major problem. The people and leaders were distracted by the surrounding enemy nations and kings who were making threatening statements. Their gods were fierce-looking, and their armies had won battles. They were definitely distractions.

The larger Northern Kingdom of Israel had been destroyed in 722 BC by the Assyrians. Now tiny Judah is called "Israel." To break through to the minds of the people, God's prophet Jeremiah used an attention-getting device: "Hear what the LORD says to you, people of Israel" (Jeremiah 10:1). He's saying, "Get your attention off your neighbors and put it on God!"

The other nations were terrified of the weather, the sun, and the stars because their gods allegedly communicated with them through those signs in the heavens. But the Lord God said their pagan gods were "like a scarecrow in a cucumber field, their idols cannot speak" (verse 5). In other words, "Don't fear them because they can't talk, walk, or do anything." Rather, "Look to the King of the nations! Give Him your full attention and listen. All the other leaders and their nations are foolish because they listen to worthless idols" (Jeremiah 10:7-8).

Today people make other things their gods, such as money, sex, alcohol, power, possessions, drugs, independence, and so forth. What pathetic, puny gods! There is no one like our God! Listen only to Him.

Question for Today: Does the King of the nations have your attention? What distractions try to keep your focus turned away from Him?

Prayer: Majestic King of the nations, no one compares with You. You are all-powerful and wise. I want to keep my ears open to Your leading regardless of what confronts me. You're awesome in every way.

Eternal King
An Argument Against Serving Dead Wood

*The LORD is the true God; he is the living God, the
eternal King. When he is angry, the earth trembles; the
nations cannot endure his wrath (Jeremiah 10:10).*

FYI: The Israelites had turned away from God and worshipped a wide
variety of idols, including *Chemosh*, the chief and "detestable god" of
Moab (1 Kings 11:7). They also served the fertility god *Baal* (Jeremiah
7:9); *Ashtoreth*, "the vile goddess of the Sidonians" (2 Kings 23:13); and
sacrificed their children to Molek, the despicable god of the Ammonites (2 Kings 23:10).

Jeremiah gives a long list of the characteristics of these idols in Jeremiah 10
and compares them with the Lord God. Idols can't speak, move, or walk.
Since they're just dead wood dressed up with silver and gold, they are
unable to help or harm anyone. The people who worship them are sense-
less and foolish (Jeremiah 10:8-9). Totally different than these false gods,
the Lord God is great and mighty in power (verse 6). He is the King of
the nations (verse 7).

On top of all that, the Lord is the true God, not some man-made idol.
He is the living God, not some hunk of gold-plated, dead wood. To con-
clude his argument, Jeremiah declares that the Lord is the eternal King
who rules the universe forever, including all the detestable idols. Given
who the true God is, why would you want to serve the gods of this world?

Question for Today: Why do you want to worship the eternal King and
not the false gods that clamor for your attention?

Prayer: Eternal King, the facts are overwhelming. You are the true and living God. There is no one like You anywhere in the universe. I worship You
alone! I want people to know that You, the living God, still reign supreme.

LORD God Almighty
Tasty Words

When your words came, I ate them; they were
my joy and my heart's delight, for I bear your
name, LORD God Almighty (Jeremiah 15:16).

FYI: LORD God Almighty is a combination of *Jehovah*, *Elohim*, and *Tsebaoth*: *Jehovah-Elohim-Tsebaoth*. Jeremiah followed God's direction even though every time he spoke His words the Israelites rejected them. Sometimes they beat God's prophet and threw him into prison (Jeremiah 37:15-16). During the 40 years Jeremiah prophesied, the Bible gives no indication that anyone came to the Lord. In fact, after the destruction of Jerusalem by the Babylonians in 522 BC, some of the remaining Israelites in Judah disobeyed God's command to stay in Israel, and headed to Egypt. They kidnapped Jeremiah and took him with them (Jeremiah 43:1-7). But Jeremiah didn't get discouraged. He kept trusting God.

Close your eyes and think of your favorite food. Imagine having someone serve it to you. It looks so delicious and smells so delightful. You can almost taste it. Getting hungry? Now, suppose a friend told you his favorite food was considered by most people to be inedible. What would your reaction be if he told you his special food was words? You'd probably think, "He's crazy!"

God's prophet Jeremiah ate the Lord God Almighty's words and liked them. Interestingly, that wasn't his first reaction. When the words of the Lord first came to him: "I appointed you as a prophet to the nations," Jeremiah responded, "Alas, Sovereign LORD...I do not know how to speak; I am too young" (Jeremiah 1:6). But then "the LORD reached out his hand and touched my mouth and said to me, 'I have put my words in your mouth'" (verse 9). Years later (as noted in today's verse), Jeremiah testified that God's words became his joy and the delight of his life. What a change!

The Lord God Almighty's words give life and hope regardless of the attitudes of other people. When we eat God's words by studying, pondering, and acting on their wisdom, we're changed for the better.

Question for Today: Have you tasted God's Word? Is it your delight? It is God's food for you. Eat up!

Prayer: Lord God Almighty, Your Word builds me up and causes me to reach out to others with Your love. Help me to study the Bible more consistently so I can share Your tasty word with people who need to know about Your goodness. Fill me with Your joy.

Sovereign LORD
Tears and Praise

The Sovereign LORD is my strength; he makes my feet like the feet of a deer, he enables me to tread on the heights (Habakkuk 3:19).

FYI: "Sovereign LORD" is *Adonai-Jehovah*. "The feet of a deer" refers to mountain gazelles that are swift and sure-footed so they can escape predators. They symbolize confidence and trust in the faithful, Sovereign Lord who gives strength and comfort to those who run to Him for help.

How do you react when your most important desire is dashed? What is your response when a coveted position in your company that you've been working toward for years is given to someone else? Or perhaps an accident has suddenly taken the life of your close friend? Or maybe your loved one just got test results back that shows he or she has advanced cancer?

When this happens, what is your usual reaction? Do you complain to others? Do you lash out? Do you feel sorry for yourself? Do you cry out angrily, "God, where are You?" The prophet Habakkuk received a terrifying vision from the Sovereign Lord. God had been telling His people in Judah to serve and obey Him. However, they continually committed abominable sins—for more than 300 years. The day of reckoning was coming. God told Habakkuk that the ferocious Babylonians were coming to attack Judah (Habakkuk 1:6-11).

Shocked, saddened, bewildered—Habakkuk felt all these emotions. Finally he said, basically, "Even if You, Lord, allow the annihilation of everything I know and love, yet I will be joyful in God my Savior" (Habakkuk 3:17-18). Bad things will happen to everyone, and in this world all living things die. But the people who put their trust in the Sovereign Lord will receive strength to handle the losses and even praise God in the midst of their tears. God is always in control—even during our darkest days.

Question for Today: What is your response to devastated hopes and crushed dreams?

Prayer: Sovereign LORD, I don't like pain and anguish. I pray I will cling to You no matter what hits me. Help me praise You in all circumstances.

God of My Ancestors
Great Stories from the Past

*I thank and praise you, God of my ancestors: You
have given me wisdom and power, you have made
known to me what we asked of you, you have made
known to us the dream of the king (Daniel 2:23).*

FYI: This is the only time "God of my ancestors" appears in the Bible.

In 605 BC, King Nebuchadnezzar conquered Jerusalem and sent many of the captives to Babylon, including young Daniel and three of his friends. Still Daniel praised the "God of my ancestors." He undoubtedly knew the powerful stories of his godly ancestors, including Abraham, Joseph, Moses, David, and Elijah. They all trusted God to do great things.

Daniel, in training to be the king's servant, was presented with an incredible challenge. The king had experienced a dream and wanted his advisors to tell him what the dream was and what it meant. If they failed, he would kill them all, including Daniel and his friends (Daniel 2:1-13).

When Daniel heard about the situation, he immediately turned to the "God of my ancestors" to reveal to him the king's dream and its interpretation. He knew that the same God who changes the seasons and sets up kings and takes down kings could describe the dream and relay its meaning (Daniel 2:19-23). And God came through. Daniel told the king the dream and its interpretation.

The Lord gave Daniel exactly what he needed—wisdom and power and courage. God is great! All believers in Jesus, whether Jewish or not, are descendants of Abraham through their faith (Romans 4:1; Galatians 3:6-7; James 2:21). So we too can pray to the "God of my ancestors."

Question for Today: What kind of impact have your ancestors had on you? What kind of impact do you want to have on the next generation?

Prayer: God of my ancestors, I praise You for all You've done through believers in the past. I pray You'll do great things in and through me so I can show and tell the next generation how wonderful You are.

Lord of Kings
Predicting Future World Empires

*The king said to Daniel, "Surely your God is the God of
gods and the Lord of kings and a revealer of mysteries, for
you were able to reveal this mystery" (Daniel 2:47).*

FYI: This is the only time "Lord of kings" appears in the Bible. Nebuchadnezzar's dream was of a giant statue. Daniel explained that the statue represented empires: Babylon was the head of gold, Medo-Persia was the chest and arms of silver, Greece was the belly and thighs of bronze, Rome was the legs of iron, and the iron/clay feet were divisions of the Roman Empire (Daniel 2:26-46).

Mysteries intrigue us. As we watch detectives in a movie frantically search for killers, we try to unravel the plot so we can predict what happened and who committed the crime. At the end of the show, the mystery is solved and the perpetrator is captured. There is a sense of relief and closure when the puzzle is solved.

But what about a mysterious nightmare you can't figure out? That's what happened to King Nebuchadnezzar. None of his advisors could interpret his mysterious dream (Daniel 2:10-11). However, Daniel courageously stated, "No wise man, enchanter, magician or diviner can explain to the king the mystery he has asked about, but there is a God in heaven who reveals mysteries" (verses 27-28). Daniel then relayed what God had told him about the king's dream.

Nebuchadnezzar enthusiastically exclaimed that Daniel's God revealed mysteries and was greater than the idols the Babylonians worshiped. "Your God is the 'Lord of kings'," he said, meaning Daniel's God was the master of all the kings who would rule the world kingdoms to come.

Question for Today: Are you trusting the Lord of kings to give you courage to help others know Him?

Prayer: Magnificent Lord of kings, You rule over all the political leaders and countries in our world. I give praise and honor to You. Guide me so I can make You known to my family and friends.

Portion of Jacob
You Chose Me and I Choose You

He who is the Portion of Jacob is not like these, for
he is the Maker of all things, including the
people of his inheritance (Jeremiah 51:19).

FYI: "Portion of Jacob" is used twice—in today's verse and in Jeremiah 10:16. The word "portion" is used 95 times. In addition to the two passages in Jeremiah, it refers to the Lord only in Psalm 16:5; 73:26; 119:57; 142:5; Lamentations 3:24.

"That one is yours, and this one is mine." That could be two people dividing up chess pieces before they play a game or it could be said about the last two slices of a birthday cake. Hopefully the division is fair for each person. If not, an argument may ensue. But what if one person chooses and the other person can't debate the outcome? That may seem awkward—but not if the one choosing is God.

The Lord is the Maker of all things, and He chose Jacob (the people of Israel) as His inheritance (Deuteronomy 32:9). The Lord is Jacob's Portion. He is not like the lifeless chunks of wood, metal, and stone idols that can't help anyone. The Portion of Jacob is alive and involved, having created everything. With the psalmist, we can shout, "My flesh and my heart may fail, but God is the strength of my heart and my portion forever" (Psalm 73:26). Consider the benefits of having the Lord Almighty as your portion.

Question for Today: Is the Portion of Jacob the God you choose to worship?

Prayer: Portion of Jacob, I wholeheartedly choose You. I want to love and obey You.

God of Retribution
Judgment for the Arrogant

A destroyer will come against Babylon; her warriors will be captured, and their bows will be broken. For the LORD is a God of retribution; he will repay in full (Jeremiah 51:56).

FYI: Babylon is prominent in the Bible. It's mentioned numerous times. In the book of Revelation, Babylon is a symbol of great rebellion and defiance against God (Revelation 14:8; 16:19; 17:5; 18:2,10,21).

Just about every news program includes reports of innocent people having been killed or harmed. Wars, murders, robberies, swindles, rapes, assaults, bullying, and hundreds of other crimes victimize people every day.

When violence happens to us, it becomes an even more gut-wrenching reality. And when the savvy perpetrators get away with their crimes, it really galls us. We ask, "Where is justice?" "How can this be made right?" There is only One being capable of righteous judgment and recompense—the God of retribution. We live in an immoral world, and nothing gets by God. He is righteous, holy, and just. Nations may ignore Him or vigorously oppose Him, but they do so at their peril.

From 626 to 539 BC, Babylon was the greatest world power. With arrogance the Babylonians sacked nations and murdered millions. In 586 BC, for the third and final time, King Nebuchadnezzar conquered Jerusalem, totally destroyed the Jewish temple, and deported many Israelites to Babylon. The Lord, the God of retribution, promised He would punish Babylon (Jeremiah 51:57-58). Yes, God is merciful and gives multiple opportunities for repentance, but when His kindness and grace are consistently spurned, He brings judgment. Babylon wouldn't listen, so in 539 BC, King Cyrus of Persia fulfilled Jeremiah's prophesy and totally destroyed Babylon.

Question for Today: Why do you think God punished Babylon so severely?

Prayer: God of retribution, thank You for being merciful yet holy. I humble myself before You and ask You to forgive me for my pride and selfishness.

David
David Reigns Forever

*They will serve the LORD their God and David their
king, whom I will raise up for them (Jeremiah 30:9).*

FYI: King David is greatly revered in the Bible; his name occurs 1,092 times. Check out these passages that show that Jesus is the fulfillment of all the promises God made to David, including that one of his offspring would rule the world eternally: Isaiah 55:3-4; Ezekiel 34:24-25; 37:24-25; Hosea 3:5; Matthew 22:42-46; Acts 2:22-36.

You can have multiple identities at the same time. You can be the child of your parents, the graduate of a certain school, the spouse of your partner, and the parent of your child. Each identity requires a different skill set and includes different responsibilities. A person has several identities, but he or she is still the same person. However, no one can have two distinct personages—with one exception. When Jeremiah wrote about David, the monarch had been dead more than 400 years. The first identity of David was as the greatest king and hero of Israel, even though he was imperfect and sinful. The second identity for David would be as king and ruler from David's throne forever (Ezekiel 37:24-25).

In that sense, Jesus Christ, our Lord, *is* the second David. He lived on this earth and died, but unlike the first David, who stayed in the grave, the perfect and sinless second David was raised to life and given the honor of sitting on the everlasting throne promised to David's descendants.

The apostle Peter proclaimed to the Israelites, "God has made this Jesus, whom you crucified, both Lord and Messiah" (Acts 2:36). Jesus is both human and divine—Son of David and Sovereign Lord forever.

Question for Today: What do you think about the concept of first and second Davids?

Prayer: Eternal King David, Your love for me and others is thrilling. You came to earth to die and opened the way for me to come into right relationship with God. Rule in my heart, and show me how to help others to know You.

Most High God
Now the Whole World Knows

It is my pleasure to tell you about the miraculous
signs and wonders that the Most High God
has performed for me (Daniel 4:2).

FYI: "Most High God" means there is no other god or anything in the universe that even comes close to Him. This expression is found seven times in the Bible, four of them being in the book of Daniel (3:26; 4:2; 5:18,21). The other times are Mark 5:7; Luke 8:28; Acts 16:17.

When a baby comes into the world, the parents want everyone to know. Baby pictures on their social media pages show the world the new addition to their family. They tweet their friends the good news. They want the whole world to share in their joy. Other people often broadcast their struggles, heartaches, disappointments, and even declining health situations.

Such communications in ancient days were very limited. Amazingly, King Nebuchadnezzar of Babylon wrote a letter proclaiming the Most High God "to the nations and peoples of every language, who live in all the earth" (Daniel 4:1). The king's story is compelling even though it was written more than 2,500 years ago. As the ruler of the largest kingdom of the known world, with millions of people under his authority, he was "contented and prosperous" (verse 4). Then one night he had a dream that terrified him, so he asked his advisors to tell him what it was and to give their interpretation (verses 6-7). Daniel talked with God and then went to the king with God's reply (verse 8). Daniel was terrified because he was going to have to deliver bad news.

The dream foretold Nebuchadnezzar's fall. For seven years he would experience the humiliation of living like a wild animal because he was arrogant and prideful. The dream came true, and Nebuchadnezzar ate grass like an ox until he acknowledged that the God in heaven rules (verse 36). When he became a humble man, his kingdom was restored. That's when he wrote the letter giving honor and praise to the Most High God.

Question for Today: Have you written to others about how the Most High God changed your life?

Prayer: I humble myself before You, Most High God. My prideful attitudes and selfishness offend You. Forgive me for trying to control my life. I love You and want to serve You with my entire being.

King of Heaven
Changes in a Proud Man

*Now I, Nebuchadnezzar, praise and exalt and glorify
the King of heaven, because everything he does is
right and all his ways are just. And those who walk
in pride he is able to humble (Daniel 4:37).*

FYI: This is the only time "King of heaven" appears. God is also referred to as "King of all the earth" (Psalm 47:7), "King of glory" (Psalm 24:7), "King of Israel" (Zephaniah 3:15), "King of kings and Lord of lords" (Revelation 19:16), "King of the Jews" (Matthew 2:2), and "King of the nations" (Jeremiah 10:7).

Reflect on your life. Was there a time when you didn't know God as your Savior and Lord? What did you think or do that showed any selfishness and pride? Do you remember the problems you encountered because you tried to control your life and do as you pleased? How did you handle your sins and guilt?

Now think about how you found out about the Lord God. Why did you choose to humble yourself before the King of heaven and ask for His forgiveness of your sins? Look at your life right now. What changes has He made in you? If you want an example of how to do all this, read Nebuchadnezzar's letter to the known world at the time. He experienced the truth of the saying, "There is only one God, and I am not Him." Oh, Nebuchadnezzar thought he was for a time. He bragged, "Is not this the great Babylon I have built as the royal residence, by my mighty power and for the glory of my majesty?" (Daniel 4:30).

Because of his prideful attitude, arrogance, and self-centeredness, God took away his kingdom and his sanity, causing the king to live like a wild animal for seven years (verses 31-33). Finally, the man humbled himself before the Most High God, honoring and glorifying Him who lives forever (verse 34).

Nebuchadnezzar had intellectually called Daniel's God the "God of gods and the Lord of kings and a revealer of mysteries" (Daniel 2:47). But now, with all humility, the king calls God "King of heaven." And God restored him to his throne.

Nebuchadnezzar finally recognized that he was king of Babylon only, a puny world kingdom that was his only because the King of heaven had given it to him. The King of heaven ruled over him, his kingdom, the earth, and all of heaven. Nebuchadnezzar now knew who was really in control and, with deepest gratitude, he praised, exalted, and glorified Him.

Question for Today: How did you finally realize that God is God and you are not?

Prayer: Praise and glory are Yours, King of heaven. Your mighty kingdom endures forever. You lift up the humble. My deepest desire is to honor You with my whole life. Praise Your mighty name!

Breath of the Almighty
The Origin of Life

The Spirit of God has made me; the breath of
the Almighty gives me life (Job 33:4).

FYI: This is the only time the name "breath of the Almighty" appears in the Bible. In today's verse, the word "Spirit" means "wind" or "breath." Other references to times the Spirit of God gave life are found in Genesis 2:7; Job 32:8; Ezekiel 37:9; John 3:8; 20:22; Romans 8:6,10.

You've probably heard the idiom "breathe life into..." It means to infuse new energy and vitality into something that's struggling, dying, or dead. If your flowers are drooping, you can "breathe life" into them by watering them. In football, people say, "The new quarterback breathed life into the floundering team." That expression originated in the Bible. In fact, it comes from the book of Job, which contains poetry going back to the time of Abraham. The Holy Spirit is a member of the Trinity, equal in every way to God the Father and God the Son. The Spirit was actively engaged in the creation of the world (Genesis 1:2). The Spirit is called the "breath of the Almighty" because He emanates from God and gives life. The Holy Spirit gave life to the pile of dirt God formed into Adam. The Spirit came sounding like the blowing of a violent wind and filled the disciples at Pentecost (Acts 2:2). In fact, all the biblical authors were inspired by the Holy Spirit to write God's Word (2 Timothy 3:16).

All humanity is born with a fallen nature inherited from Adam. God considered us dead spiritually (Ephesians 2). But when we put our faith in Jesus Christ, the Holy Spirit gives us new birth (John 3:8). Just like the Spirit breathed life into Adam, He breathes life into you and me—eternal life.

Question for Today: Has the breath of the Almighty given you new life?

Prayer: Dear God, Your grace is so great that You offered me new life through the breath of the Almighty. I will eternally praise You.

Ancient of Days
The Fearsome Four Meet Their Match

*As I looked, thrones were set in place, and the Ancient of
Days took his seat. His clothing was as white as snow; the
hair of his head was white like wool. His throne was flaming
with fire, and its wheels were all ablaze (Daniel 7:9).*

FYI: "Ancient of Days" appears three times in God's Word, and all are
in Daniel 7. Some other fabulous descriptions of our splendid God
and His throne are found in Isaiah 6:1-4; Ezekiel 1:3-28; Revelation 4–20.

Take a moment to imagine what God looks like. Many people, when
asked this question, draw a blank. Throughout biblical history, only a few
people have claimed to actually *see* God. When Moses met with the Lord
at the burning bush, he was afraid to look on God so he closed his eyes
(Exodus 3:6). When the Lord showed His presence to Moses, He only
allowed him to see His back so Moses wouldn't die (Exodus 33:21-23).
One of the few who saw God and wrote about it was Daniel. Through a
dramatic vision, God revealed to Daniel a future when four kings would
rise up to conquer and rule the world. These were represented by four terrifying and fierce beasts—a lion with wings, a bear, a leopard with four
wings and four heads, and a beast with iron teeth and ten horns with eyes
and a mouth (Daniel 7:2-8). These beasts were extremely ferocious and
hideous in destroying the other nations. But then, like a spotlight shifting
to light up a different entity, a magnificent being came on stage who was
totally different than the four world-conquering beasts.

Suddenly, the Ancient of Days, the splendid, eternal God, took His
seat to judge the world. The horrifying beasts are the four kings who
destroyed nations and ruled the world, but God, the Ancient of Days, is
the Judge of world rulers. Nothing on earth resembles Him or His judgment seat.

Amazingly, the Ancient of Days gives absolute authority to "one like
a son of man" (a human being) to dominate the world rulers and set up
His eternal kingdom. This futuristic scene in heaven predicts the coming
of the Lord Jesus Christ to rule the world (Revelation 19–22). For thousands of years the beasts will dominate all nations, but one day the Ancient

of Days will send the Son of Man to violently slay the beasts and take His place on His eternal throne over all.

Question for Today: Do you yearn for the day when the Son of Man will conquer the beasts that rule the natural world?

Prayer: Magnificent Ancient of Days, come and set up Your judgment seat. Send the Lord Jesus Christ to conquer the ungodly nations. Please do it soon.

Prince of Princes
Christ vs. Antichrist

*A fierce-looking king, a master of intrigue, will arise…He
will cause deceit to prosper, and he will consider himself
superior. When they feel secure, he will destroy many and
take his stand against the Prince of princes. Yet he will be
destroyed, but not by human power (Daniel 8:23,25).*

FYI: In the Bible, the word "prince" appears 100 times referring to
human beings. In addition, 7 times the word refers to Satan (Matthew 9:34; 12:24; Mark 3:22; Luke 11:15; John 12:31; 14:30; 16:11), 3 times to
Michael the archangel (Daniel 10:13,20; 12:1), and 3 times to Jesus (Isaiah 9:6; Daniel 8:25; Acts 5:31).

All people dream while sleeping. Some people say we dream many dreams
each night, but most of us remember very few of them. For dreams, the
brain picks fragments of our experiences and puts them together in strange,
seemingly illogical ways. We might have recurring, or similar patterned,
dreams. Some dreams can be so vivid and realistic that we're not sure if we
were asleep or awake.

Nightmares can wake us up in the middle of the night, making us feel
distressed, anxious, and even terrified. Maybe we envision something so
unpleasant and frightful that it greatly upsets us. Then for the next few
minutes, hours, or days we constantly think about it, wondering what it
means.

That's a little like how Daniel probably felt after God gave him visions
predicting specific, horrible, future events. Daniel wrote about the visions
God gave him regarding the Babylonian and Persian empires. The dreams
weren't horrible nightmares, but they were of specific events that would
happen. One vision depicted a two-horned ram that represented the kings
of the Medes and Persians. The shaggy goat with horns represented the
kings of the Greek Empire, with one fierce-looking king who would cause
astounding devastation and destroy Israel (Daniel 8:23-24). That king's
downfall would come when he fought against the Prince of princes.

This and other visions recorded in the book of Daniel are "historical
prophesies," meaning the predicted events actually happened. But they

are also prophesies of greater future events. For instance, around 600 BC, Daniel wrote about the Greek Empire. Alexander the Great didn't conquer Jerusalem until 332 BC! The fierce-looking king was Antiochus IV Epiphanies, who desecrated the Jewish temple around 167 BC. This king is a prophetic forerunner of the Antichrist, who will battle the Prince of princes (a messianic title for Jesus Christ).

Jesus will defeat His archenemy during the great tribulation spoken of in the book of Revelation. Our regal, supreme Prince is the all-conquering hero of history!

Question for Today: Do you have a recurring dream? What do you think it means?

Prayer: No one, not even the powerful Antichrist, can defeat You, Prince of princes. You conquer *all* Your enemies. Give me the courage and wisdom to defeat any temptation that tries to pull me away from You.

Lord of Heaven
Mene, Mene, Tekel, Peres

*You have set yourself up against the Lord of heaven. You
had the goblets from his temple brought to you, and you
and your nobles, your wives and your concubines drank
wine from them. You praised the gods of silver and gold, of
bronze, iron, wood and stone, which cannot see or hear
or understand. But you did not honor the God who holds
in his hand your life and all your ways (Daniel 5:23).*

FYI: God reveals His name "Lord of heaven" only this one time. Daniel tells the greatest king in the world at the time that *Adonai* is the supreme owner and ruler of heaven, as well as everything on earth. Even today "the handwriting on the wall" means the threat of coming doom or the tragic end of something.

More than 500 years later, Jesus adds to this great name by calling His Father "Lord of heaven and earth" (Matthew 11:25; Luke 10:21). God is in control over everything, even the distribution of knowledge. To complete the revelation of "Lord of heaven and earth," Paul declares to the Athenians that no idol can compare to God because He is supreme over everything on earth and in the heavens (Acts 17:24).

King Belshazzar, son of Nebuchadnezzar, arrogantly honored his Babylonian gods and demonstrated his disdain for the Most High God that his father had humbly praised. In the midst of a lavish banquet put on by Belshazzar and attended by more than a thousand nobles, suddenly fingers of a human hand appeared and wrote these words on the palace wall: "*Mene, Mene, Tekel, Parsin*" (Daniel 5:1-12,25).

The banquet atmosphere became tense. King Belshazzar was so terrified his knees were knocking. None of the enchanters, astrologers, and diviners could read or interpret the cryptic words. The commotion caused the queen to come in. She reminded Belshazzar that Daniel had been greatly honored by Nebuchadnezzar because he interpreted his dream. Daniel was quickly summoned to interpret these mysterious words (Daniel 5:13-22).

Daniel courageously spoke directly to the king. "You, a mere man, have elevated your tiny, lifeless gods made of earthly materials above the Lord of Heaven who rules all of heaven and is supreme king of all kingdoms on earth. *Mene, Mene, Tekel, Peres* (*Peres* is the singular of *Parsin*) meant God has numbered the days of your reign and brought it to an end. You have been weighed on the scales and found wanting. Your kingdom is divided and given to the Medes and Persians" (Daniel 5:26-28).

Belshazzar discovered that mankind may challenge God's authority or minimize His existence, but in the end we all will bow before His throne. God had demonstrated His grace and forgiveness to Nebuchadnezzar, but his son refused to humble himself. That very night Babylon was destroyed and Belshazzar was killed. The prophecy was fulfilled. The Lord of heaven is supreme and holds each person's life in His hands.

Question for Today: Are you humbly praising and honoring the Lord of heaven?

Prayer: How I praise and honor You, Lord of heaven. There is no one like You in the universe. Thank You that my life and ways are in Your hands. I trust You to empower me to serve You well.

God of Daniel
Standing Up to Kings and Lions

[King Darius wrote,] "I issue a decree that in every part of my kingdom people must fear and reverence the God of Daniel. For he is the living God and he endures forever; his kingdom will not be destroyed, his dominion will never end" (Daniel 6:26).

FYI: This is the only reference to "God of Daniel." Darius the Mede was most likely the name Daniel used for Gobryas, the general who captured Babylon (Daniel 5:30-31). Darius was made ruler of the old Babylonian kingdom by Cyrus the Great (9:1).

If you asked 100 people, "What is God like?" you'd probably get 100 different answers. Many would likely say that no one can really know if God exists. Since most who give that reply don't read the Bible for the answer, how will they know God is real and what He is like? The fact is, *you* may be the only "Bible" the nonbelievers in your circle of friends will read. When they look at your life, what kind of a God do they see?

King Darius was duped by his *satraps* (governors) to make a law that made it illegal to pray to any god but him for thirty days (Daniel 6:7). Daniel defied the law and continued to pray to the one true God. After Daniel's arrest for breaking the law, he was thrown into a den of lions. Daniel survived because he trusted God, who sent an angel to shut the mouths of the lions (Daniel 6:6-22).

The only understanding Darius had of God was by observing Daniel. The God of Daniel was alive and active—not dead like the idols worshipped by all the others in the kingdom. Darius knew from observation that the "God of Daniel" was the everlasting Ruler of all kingdoms, and One who responds to the prayers of those who trust Him (Daniel 6:27).

Question for Today: When people observe your life, do they see your God?

Prayer: How alive and powerful You are, God of Daniel! I pray that You will give me the strength to stand courageously for You regardless of the attitudes of the people around me.

God Most High
Choose "A" or "B"

[Israel] remembered that God was their Rock, that God Most High was their Redeemer (Psalm 78:35).

FYI: "God Most High" also occurs in Genesis 14:18-20,22; Psalm 57:2; Hosea 11:7.

Some people have a hard time making up their minds. One day they like choice "A," and the next day (or minute) they like choice "B." They constantly flip-flop between the two, never really settling on either one. The Israelites continually fluctuated between serving God and serving idols. God Most High did miracles to get them out of Egypt, but they rebelled again. The Lord brought judgment against them, and then He showed them great mercy. Still they would return to Him for a while and then reject Him again.

The nation of Israel knew God Most High. They knew He was far above any idols or mini gods. They could choose to serve Him and enjoy His mercy and love or they could choose to serve idols and live wickedly. What about believers today? How often do we vacillate between enjoying God and serving ourselves?

Question for Today: Do you flip-flop or do you faithfully serve your Redeemer?

Prayer: Oh God Most High, You are so merciful and gracious. Why do I keep vacillating between serving You and serving me? Please forgive me. I want to be consistently faithful to You. Help me love You more.

God of Justice
Danger Ahead!

*You have wearied the LORD with your words. "How have
we wearied him?" you ask. By saying, "All who do evil
are good in the eyes of the LORD, and he is pleased with
them" or "Where is the God of justice?" (Malachi 2:17).*

FYI: "God of justice" also appears in Psalm 50:6 and Isaiah 30:18.

Warning signs are posted at hazards to protect people from danger. A roadside sign warning that a dangerously sharp curve is ahead tells drivers to slow down. If they don't, they risk injury or death.

When people suffer the consequences of ignoring warning signs, they'd be foolish to blame the sign. But people often do exactly that when they suffer after rejecting warnings given by God. They often blame God for their fate. For instance, the Lord clearly says, "You shall not commit adultery" (Exodus 20:14). But many people ignore God's command and even blatantly promote adultery. When the consequences produce broken homes, violence, venereal diseases, and unwanted children who are hurt emotionally and physically, people blame God.

Many people live as if God doesn't exist and encourage others to do likewise. In their naiveté, they think that the God of justice is an obsolete concept. They choose to believe they can live the way they want without suffering any consequences. But the warning signs are posted throughout the Bible. The biblical God is the God of love, forgiveness, and mercy, but He's also the God of justice who is righteous and holy. When people violate His laws, there are inevitable, negative repercussions. Beware!

Question for Today: Have you been wearying the God of justice with your blaming Him and offering excuses and rationalizations?

Prayer: God of justice, You are merciful and gracious. In Your great love for me, You've given me warnings so I won't experience the consequences of doing foolish and even evil things. Help me do what is right in Your sight.

God of Heaven
Keep On Keeping On

[Nehemiah] said: "LORD, the God of heaven, the great and awesome God, who keeps his covenant of love with those who love him and keep his commandments..." (Nehemiah 1:5).

FYI: Jesus taught a parable "to show [His disciples] that they should always pray and not give up" (Luke 18:1). Considering his commitment to rebuilding the wall around Jerusalem, it's amazing that Nehemiah had probably never been there before.

There are times when it seems like our prayers aren't being answered or that maybe God hasn't heard them. We pray and pray, but nothing happens. During these "dry" times, we often give up. Day after day goes by without anything changing. We get tired and skip some days. Then one day we realize it's been two weeks since we prayed. Discouragement has led to forgetfulness.

Nehemiah had a different perspective. Jerusalem had been destroyed in 586 BC, and, in about 444 BC, Nehemiah heard about the deplorable state of the Jewish inhabitants and the city itself (Nehemiah 1:1-3). What could he do? He was a Jewish exile more than 1,000 miles away. On top of that, he was the cupbearer for the Persian king Artaxerxes I.

Not being able to talk directly with the king for fear that he would be displeased and have him killed, Nehemiah kept his burden to himself. He fasted, mourned, and prayed to the Lord for the Jews and Jerusalem during the month of Kislev (November–December). He continued faithfully until the month of Nisan (March–April) (Nehemiah 2:1). That was four months of intense, intercessory prayer. Why did he keep seeking the God of heaven? Because he knew that the Lord keeps His promises. Nehemiah knew God answers prayers in His time and in His way.

We must never give up praying, continuing until God answers.

Question for Today: What are you trusting the Lord to do even though it feels like your prayers are unheard?

Prayer: God of heaven, You are great and awesome. Your covenant of love never stops. My desire is to pray more and trust You for amazing blessings. Help me be more consistent in talking with You.

Word
Are You Listening?

In the beginning was the Word, and the Word was
with God, and the Word was God (John 1:1).

FYI: God communicated directly to people about Himself and His will in hundreds of ways. For instance, the phrases "word of the Lord" occurs 240 times, "word of God" appears 46 times, "God's word" is given 6 times, and "LORD's word(s)" comes 5 times.

Our lives are built on words. It's difficult to imagine a world without them. Why? Because that's the way we communicate and relate. Words give meaning to life and build our awareness of how other people are thinking, feeling, and behaving.

Think about the problem God had. He is Spirit and lives in eternal glory. After He created the universe by speaking words (Psalm 33:6), God created human beings. How could He communicate with them? Maybe He could have talked to them through flashes of light or the sounds of animals. But He didn't. God chose words as the vehicle to relate to Adam and Eve. He spoke words that they understood and could speak back to Him. He spoke in such a way that people using any language could understand Him. He revealed His law and His will about how people should live to please Him. He sent prophets, did miracles, and worked through godly leaders. Unfortunately, the majority of mankind rebelled and rejected Him. They killed His prophets, forgot His miracles, and disobeyed His leaders.

So let's make our communication supremely clear: God sent His Son, Jesus, to earth. Jesus is God in the flesh. He is the embodiment of God's message to us. Jesus is *the Word*, the eternal God. Do you want to know what God's will is? Listen to the Word—Jesus. Do you desire to know God better? Look to the Word—Jesus Christ. Are you curious about the future of the world? Believe the Word—Jesus. Without Him there would be no world (verse 3), and without Him there would be no life (John 1:3-4). Jesus is the exact representation of God. He is the clearest communicator of who God really is in all His glory (Hebrews 1:2-3).

Question for Today: Are you listening to the Word or to the world?

Prayer: Jesus, You are the Word, the greatest communicator of God because You are God. I want to learn more about You. Help me understand what You reveal about Yourself. Teach me all I need to know to be someone who honors You.

Son of the Most High
Saying "Yes" to the Most High

*He will be great and will be called the Son of
the Most High. The Lord God will give him the
throne of his father David (Luke 1:32).*

FYI: This is the only time in the Bible that the name "Son of the Most High" is revealed. It's such a special name that only Jesus can be called it. Isn't it amazing that God entrusted the birth of His Son to a teenage girl from a family of humble means?

Do you like surprises? Especially really good, big surprises that wow you, such as a surprise birthday party with all your friends there? You weren't expecting it, so you were probably momentarily confused by all the people. Then you broke out into laughter and smiled until the muscles in your face hurt. You felt loved, accepted, treasured, and honored.

Can you imagine how Mary felt when the angel came and made his sudden announcement? Gabriel went to her and told her that she would bear the most unusual child the world had ever seen. In fact, He would not be fathered by a human, but by the power of the Most High God.

At first Mary was confused. After all, she'd never had sexual relations with a man. She could easily have exclaimed, "That's impossible!" Certainly her culture didn't look kindly upon young, unwed, pregnant women. Mary, probably a teenager, was startled and afraid.

Gabriel told Mary that Jesus would be called the "Son of the Most High." The Greek form of the adjective translated "high," *hypsistou*, literally means "the heights." Gospel writer Luke is showing the authority that Jesus and God the Father share. Gabriel told Mary that God would give His Son the royal, eternal throne of David. In other words, her Son would be the true King of humans on earth—forever.

How did Mary respond to this news of bearing a king? She said she was God's servant (*doulé*, in the New Testament Greek, which literally means to "tie oneself to another"). Trusting in God to do the impossible was only possible because Mary was bound to God. This is what enabled her to say yes to bearing Jesus and to trust God as the highest authority in her life.

Notice that Mary said "yes" to Most High's plan no matter what that might mean for her future. "I am the Lord's servant," she replied (Luke 1:38). In so saying, she wasn't putting her trust in people or other earthly substitutes for God.

Question for Today: What is God asking you to say yes to today? Perhaps to do what He is asking, you must be God's *doulé*. You must be tied to God. Are you willing?

Prayer: Son of the Most High, thank You for being King of my life. Please help me tie myself to You so that I can be open to saying yes to Your directions. Forgive me for saying no to Your plans even as I ask You to say yes to mine.

Lord's Messiah
God Finally Spoke

*It had been revealed to [Simeon] by the Holy
Spirit that he would not die before he had
seen the Lord's Messiah (Luke 2:26).*

FYI: This is the only time "Lord's Messiah" appears in the Bible, but the word "Messiah" is found 70 times in the New Testament. Jesus warned of future impostor messiahs (Matthew 24:24; Mark 13:21-22).

Do you ever feel as if God is hard to reach or unaware of your circumstances? The Bible is silent regarding the 400 years between when the Old Testament stops and the New Testament begins. We know from history that Israel was weak militarily and subjugated by a series of military and political powers, including Persia, Greece, and Rome. The Israelites chafed under these Gentile oppressors and desperately wanted freedom. They were independent for a short time, but the Roman general Pompey conquered Jerusalem in 63 BC and set up a "Roman client state."

Then the New Testament starts with the angel Gabriel speaking to Zechariah about a future son (John the Baptist) and then to Mary about her Son, Jesus. God also spoke to a devout man named Simeon, saying that he would see the "consolation of Israel," the coming of the Messiah (Luke 2:25). Because Simeon was led by the Spirit, he knew immediately when he saw the 40-day-old infant carried into the temple by his parents that this child was the fulfillment of the promise made by the Sovereign Lord.

The prophet Isaiah predicted that someday a baby would be born and be called "Wonderful Counselor, Mighty God, Everlasting Father, Prince of Peace" (Isaiah 9:6). More than 700 years later, Simeon was looking at the prophesied Messiah! Can you imagine how thrilled he must have been? Simeon enthusiastically praised the Sovereign Lord for providing salvation to the Gentiles and to the glory of the Israelites (Luke 2:29-32). This Baby would not be the military hero many expected, but He would be the Savior who would free people from the bondage of sin.

And someday the Lord's Messiah will come back as the "Lion of the Tribe of Judah" and conquer all His enemies (Revelation 5:5)!

This mighty God can give us power over all our sins. He can free us of our addictions and anything that enslaves us.

Question for Today: Where in your life do you need power from the Lord's Messiah to emancipate you?

Prayer: Jesus, You are the Lord's Messiah sent to set me free from sin. I praise You for providing such great salvation.

One and Only Son
The Greatest Love Gift

God so loved the world that he gave his one and
only Son, that whoever believes in him shall not
perish but have eternal life (John 3:16).

FYI: This passage is part of Christ's conversation with a distinguished man (John 3). Nicodemus was a highly ranked Pharisee and teacher. He was likely the most prominent teacher for the entire nation of Israel. He taught all the other Pharisees, and he sat on the Jewish ruling council. He should have known what Jesus was talking about, but he didn't.

The word "love" has a wide range of meanings and emotions attached to it. "I love pizza." "I love my car." "I love my dog." "I love to read." "I love my pastor." "I love my new shirt." "I love my grandfather." "I love my mother." "I love my spouse." "I love my children." "I love the Lord." No single definition of love can include the wide variety of usages. How do you show your love for each of these scenarios? There's a huge difference between showing how much you love pizza and how much you love your mother. If you know who your ultimate love is, in what ways would you demonstrate your feelings to that person? By tweet? Text message? Write on the person's social media page? Telephone? Take him or her to a movie? Send flowers? Cook a meal? Give jewelry?

Why not give what you know the person needs the most? God went beyond everything we could conceive to show His ultimate love for all people. He asked His one and only Son to die to pay the penalty for our sins. "One and only Son" means there is no one else like Jesus Christ. God displayed His supreme, passionate love for you and me so His revolutionary purpose would be done. Jesus provided the means for all sinful people (and we all have sinned—Romans 3:23) to enter a personal relationship with God. If a person believes in Christ's sacrifice, God forgives him or her and grants eternal life with Him. This is how God shows His magnificent love!

Once we've accepted Christ's death and resurrection for our sins and salvation, we get to live with Him whether we're physically alive on Earth or have died. God promises that we will have a relationship and a bond with Him that can *never* be broken—not by anything we do and not when a tombstone is erected for us. But the best news is that this bond is more than an eternal relationship. It's our hope and security that regardless of what we experience in this world, God's love for us will never cease. That is ultimate love!

Question for Today: How do you show your gratefulness for God's gift of ultimate love?

Prayer: God, thank You for giving Your one and only Son for me. I'm eternally grateful for Your ultimate love gift and Jesus' willing sacrifice. I believe in Your Son. I believe in You. Thank You for forgiving me and for giving me eternal life.

Holy One of God
Good Publicity from a Bad Source

A man...possessed by an impure spirit cried out, "What do you
want with us, Jesus of Nazareth? Have you come to destroy us?
I know who you are—the Holy One of God!" (Mark 1:23-24).

FYI: Luke 4:34 is a parallel passage to Mark 1:24. The name "Holy One of God" appears only one other time. After the less-committed followers left Him, Jesus asked His twelve disciples, "You do not want to leave too, do you?" Peter exclaimed, "We have come to believe and to know that you are the Holy One of God" (John 6:66-69).

You see them next to the cash register when you're paying for your groceries. Colorful tabloid magazines and newspapers splashed with captivating headlines that expose the latest gossip about rich and famous people. The truthfulness of the news is usually questionable, but people love to read about celebrities. When famous people are interviewed, they often show disdain for the tabloids. The source of the exposure negates the value of the publicity offered.

Have you ever been the focus of someone else's comments that you didn't appreciate? Maybe in school one of your friends blurted out your secret crush on someone. Ugh. Maybe you shared a deep secret with a group of your neighbors, and the news got out to everyone. You're embarrassed. Perhaps in front of your golf buddy another golfer jokes how he or she saw you kick a golf ball out of a bad spot when you thought nobody was looking. When your secrets are revealed, how do you react?

Have you noticed what Jesus did when that happened? When He started His ministry, very few people knew anything about Him. His teachings about the kingdom of God were stirring up attention. One Sabbath He went into a synagogue and began teaching. Suddenly a demon-possessed man in the audience shouted out, "I know who you are—the Holy One of God!" Yes, it was true, but note the source. It came from a *demon* inside the man. Satan and his demons are fallen angels. Before the universe was created, they sinned against God and were kicked out of heaven (2 Peter 2:4). They knew who Jesus of Nazareth really was, and they were His enemies.

Jesus reacted instantly. "'Be quiet!' said Jesus sternly. 'Come out of him!'" (Mark 1:25). Even though the demon exposed Jesus' deity, Jesus didn't want demons speaking for Him. Even if they told the truth, people would react negatively and, perhaps, reject their Messiah. Jesus angrily cast the demon out and amazed all the people, who quickly spread the news about Him (verses 26-28; Luke 4:34-37 relates the same incident.)

Only God is perfect and totally righteous. Jesus of Nazareth is the Holy One of God—fully man and fully God.

Question for Today: Jesus was revealed as the Holy One of God. How has that knowledge affected your life?

Prayer: Holy One of God, Your fame spreads—not by demons, but by people who love You and know You are God. I love You and know You are God. Your praise is continually on my lips and in my heart.

Spirit of Your Father
When You Don't Know What to Say

*"Do not worry about what to say or how to say it...it
will not be you speaking, but the Spirit of your Father
speaking through you" (Matthew 10:19-20).*

FYI: The Holy Spirit is God's Spirit, not a feeling or emotion. Christ
promised to send the Spirit (Advocate) from the Father to testify
about Him (John 15:26; 16:7).

People are looking at you, and you're uncomfortable. You're surrounded
by people who don't know Christ, and some seem antagonistic. They're
firing tough questions at you concerning your faith in Jesus. Your mind
goes blank, and you wonder, "What do I say?" In that critical moment,
relax. You may not have the answers in mind, but the Spirit of the Father
will work through you to convey His truths.

In today's verse, Jesus is sending His disciples out to proclaim the kingdom of heaven is near and to share what they've been given. He said some
people would dislike what they hear about their love and commitment to
Him. The same is true today. When you share your faith in the Lord with
people, they may be uninterested, defensive, or hostile. They may even
get upset at you. But you don't need to worry. The Spirit of the Father is
inside you. *You* may be at a loss for the right words, but the Holy Spirit
isn't. Pray, tell of your experiences with Christ, and let the Spirit of the
Father take care of the results.

Question for Today: What kinds of reactions do you get when you share
your story about Jesus?

Prayer: Father, I'm glad Your Spirit will speak through me to share Your
love and care.

Prophet
A Different Kind of Leader

*After the people saw the sign Jesus performed, they
began to say, "Surely this is the Prophet who
is to come into the world" (John 6:14).*

FYI: The three significant offices that the Jewish Messiah had to fulfill were king, priest, and prophet. Jesus fulfilled each of them. As "the Prophet," He taught the truth about God and prophesied about His death and resurrection (Matthew 16:21). In addition, Jesus is King of kings (1 Timothy 6:15) and High Priest (Hebrews 2:17; 4:14).

Have you been in a situation where you recognized somebody at church, at a party, or at work, but you had no clue what his or her name was? Quickly your thoughts raced through your memory to attach a name to the face in front of you. Guessing someone's name can be embarrassing, but you blurt out a name hoping you picked the correct one. Later on you feel really stupid when you discover you guessed wrong. Now, can you imagine how the people felt when they blurted out their confident guesses about who Jesus was—and they weren't correct?

When Moses was about to die, he said, "The LORD your God will raise up for you a prophet like me from among you, from your fellow Israelites" (Deuteronomy 18:15). So when thousands of people ate the food Jesus miraculously provided, they confidently exclaimed Jesus was the prophet Moses had predicted. They were correct—but Jesus was nothing like they'd envisioned.

The Israelites thought "the Prophet" would be a national political leader like Moses had been. However, Jesus came not to defeat the oppressive Romans, but to be a humble servant and die for the sins of all people so we could have a personal relationship with God. As Prophet, Jesus taught about His return (Matthew 16:27, John 14:28). Whatever Jesus said was the truth and will be fulfilled! So obey Him and trust Him to fulfill His promises to you. You'll never be embarrassed by obeying the ultimate Prophet.

Question for Today: Are there statements Jesus made that are hard for you to believe? Does that affect your faith in Him?

Prayer: Jesus, You are the Prophet sent to Earth to tell us about God and His love and purposes. Help me trust You more so that I will be among Your faithful disciples.

God's Messiah
What a Thought

"What about you?" [Jesus] asked. "Who do you say I am?" Peter answered, "God's Messiah" (Luke 9:20).

FYI: So far in the Gospels, Christ has been called "the Savior," "Christ the Lord," "the Son of the Most High," and other names that connect Him with *Yahweh* of the Old Testament. For this and for disrupting their teachings, the religious leaders were starting to hate Him. But His status as amazing Leader and Deliverer was ringing true in the hearts of some of the Jewish people. The winds of conflict were getting stronger.

Have you had a burst of insight? One of those amazing moments when finally you figured out a mystery? You may have pondered a confusing situation or real-life riddle for a long time, and then all of a sudden the answer hits you. *Aha!*

Peter had one of those moments. He'd heard Jesus teach, seen Him do amazing miracles, and walked beside Him for more than a year. The disciple had heard the cries of joy from people Jesus healed. Peter listened to the religious leaders scoff against Jesus and accuse Him of many bad things. Peter probably sometimes wondered, "Who is this man that I'm following?"

One day as Jesus and His disciples were walking along, Jesus stopped and punctuated the silence with the weight of a heavy question. He asked: "Who do the crowds say I am?" The disciples replied with a collection of diverse answers. Then it finally hit Peter. Jesus was the Messiah sent from God! How does Peter know? Christ's unfolding identity was evident through His teachings, miracles, how He treated people, deep and personal conversations, and His answers to questions from the disciples and from the religious leaders. Everything fit together. Peter knew Jesus was more than a man. He was God in person. Peter blurted out his insight: "God's Messiah."

Peter and the disciples may not have fully understood Christ's role as Messiah, but that seems understandable to us. His ability to save His people and His identity as the Christ of God is an unfolding mystery throughout time. Just like the disciples learned a little more about Christ day by day, we too can grow in our knowledge of our Lord and Savior. The more we learn about Jesus, the more we'll get bursts of insights into His character and message. We too can exclaim, "You are God's Messiah! Please save me!"

Question for Today: What are some bewildering thoughts you ponder about Jesus' identity?

Prayer: God's Messiah, thank You for overturning the world's expectations and perceptions of what it means and looks like to be God's provision for our needs. Please help me discover more about You.

Lord of the Harvest
Are You Comfortable?

[The Lord] told them, "The harvest is plentiful, but the workers are few. Ask the Lord of the harvest, therefore, to send out workers into his harvest field" (Luke 10:2).

FYI: This is the only time "Lord of the harvest" is used in the Bible. In Greek, the word translated "harvest" is *therismos*. It carries the connotation of a crop that is fully harvested. No fruit is left unpicked. No legume is left on the ground. The word connects figuratively with the final judgment, when God promises to gather up every single one of the righteous for His kingdom. With Christ's help, the disciples went out and made a difference in many lives.

Do you feel comfortable in your Christian walk? You go to a nice church, have lots of Christian friends, and participate in fun, small groups discussing the Bible and God. It's easy to be a Christian in the West, isn't it? That's how the disciples might have felt after a time. It was fun to follow the most popular man in the country. Thousands kept flocking to hear Jesus teach and get healed. But then Jesus started raising the bar for following Him. One man said he wanted to be His follower but needed to first take care of some family business. Another asked if he could say goodbye to his family first. Jesus indicated they weren't fit for serving God! Do His words seem harsh? "No one who puts a hand to the plow and looks back is fit for service in the kingdom of God" (Luke 9:62). But Jesus was making the seriousness and the sacrifice of following Him clear. To follow Him means saying "Yes!" to Him regardless of personal cost. And that's a tough task. Jesus called seventy-two disciples to leave their comfort zones and reach out to people who didn't know about Him and His message, such as the workers going out to harvest crops.

The harvest of people is ready, but who is going to do the work? Are you going to get out of your comfortable Christianity zone and do some hard work for the Lord of the harvest? People are waiting to hear the good news of Jesus Christ!

Jesus acknowledged it would be tough and rugged. He even said, "Go! I am sending you out like lambs among wolves" (Luke 10:3). The great news, however, is that when we're weak, Christ is strong. Jesus knew that if the disciples relied on their human abilities, they wouldn't succeed. God had to intervene to give strength to those who followed Him. And He still does that today.

Question for Today: What will it take for you to share your faith in Christ with someone? Do you think you're ill-equipped? Are you relying on your own abilities or on His power?

Prayer: Lord of the harvest, gather me up in Your reaping as You promised. Only with Your help can I follow You. Motivate others to come with me so we can walk with You together.

Lord of Heaven and Earth
The Joys of Coaching

At that time Jesus, full of joy through the Holy Spirit,
said, "I praise you, Father, Lord of heaven and earth,
because you have hidden these things from the wise and
learned, and revealed them to little children. Yes, Father,
for this is what you were pleased to do" (Luke 10:21).

FYI: "Lord of heaven and earth" is given only two other times—Matthew 11:25 and Acts 17:24.

If you're a parent, you know the fun of watching your children take their first steps. If you've coached a sport, you know the pride that wells up inside when one of your players makes a great play. You encouraged the right way to do something and motivated the player to take the risk. What joy when your players accomplish on their own what you taught. Jesus felt that way about His disciples.

For more than two years, the disciples followed Jesus and were content to listen to Him teach and watch Him perform miracles. Then one day Jesus sent them out to prepare the people for His coming. He gave them instructions on what to teach people. He also told His followers what to do when the people rejected them (Luke 10:1-16).

Jesus' followers returned with glowing reports. "Lord, even the demons submit to us in Your name" (Luke 10:17). The disciples had followed Jesus' instructions and accomplished great things. Most of the disciples were uneducated, but they trusted Jesus like little children trust their parents. Thrilled with the results, Jesus praised His Father. The Lord of heaven and earth empowered ordinary people to prepare the way for Him.

Today God wants to do extraordinary things through us to prepare people for accepting Him. The question is, "Are we trusting Him to use us?"

Question for Today: How is the Lord of heaven and earth empowering you to spread His message?

Prayer: How wonderful, Lord of heaven and earth, that You teach Your followers how to accomplish great things for Your kingdom. Empower me to prepare people for accepting You.

Son of David
Something to Get Excited About

The crowds that went ahead of him and those
that followed shouted, "Hosanna to the Son of
David!" "Blessed is he who comes in the name of the
Lord!" "Hosanna in the highest!" (Matthew 21:9).

FYI: The name "son of David" is used 29 times for descendants of the king. Sixteen of those times refer to Jesus. In Matthew 1:1-17, the genealogy of kings goes from Abraham through David, and from Solomon to Joseph, the earthly father of Jesus. In Luke 3:23-31, Mary's ancestry goes back through David all the way to Adam. Jesus was a physical descendant of King David. He was the "Son of David."

Parades are thrilling. Everyone is in a festive mood, laughing and straining to see the colorful marchers pass by. Fathers set their little children on their shoulders so they can see over the heads of the gawking multitudes. The bands electrify the onlookers with their loud marching music, along with drums beating cadence. There may be huge balloons floating by and animals prancing down the street. The atmosphere is charged with excitement. Something special is happening! This is not the usual routine. The crowds get into the action by shouting and waving at the marchers.

All that excitement didn't just happen. It took months to plan, prepare, and get support for the fun event.

One day a parade started up suddenly. Jesus had asked His disciples to get a donkey. The request must have seemed strange to them. Why did Jesus want one? They found the donkey, and then placed their cloaks on the donkey for Jesus to sit on. Kings and generals rode magnificent horses or took swift chariots, but Jesus was going to ride a common donkey to fulfill the prophesy of Zechariah 9:9: "Your king comes to you, righteous and victorious, lowly and riding on a donkey." A spontaneous crowd of people gathered and started to spread out their cloaks on the road before Jesus. Others spread tree branches they'd cut. Then the throng swarmed around Him, shouting and chanting, "Hosanna to the Son of David!"

"Hosanna" means "save." The Jews were oppressed and dominated by powerful Rome. King David had been the greatest warrior and king of

Israel, and he conquered all the surrounding nations. David was their national hero. Now here was his descendant who had healed lots of people and performed miracles before them. What awesome power He had! Surely He would liberate them from Rome. "Save us, King!" Even their children were ecstatic! Everyone was excited except the chief priests and teachers of the law. They wanted the celebration to cease. They asked Jesus to stop it, but He said, "I tell you...if they keep quiet, the stones will cry out" (Luke 19:39-40).

Sadly, this was the same crowd that five days later would shout, "Crucify him!"

Question for Today: Are you excited about the Son of David? Is He your Liberator?

Prayer: Hosanna, Son of David! My heart and lips shout your praises. You delivered me from the oppression of sin and Satan. Great is Your name. Hosanna!

True Vine
Abiding Is the Answer

[Jesus said,] "I am the true vine, and my
Father is the gardener" (John 15:1).

FYI: This is the only time Jesus' name "true vine" is given in the Bible. He is also referred to as the "true light" (John 1:9), the "true bread" (John 6:32), the "true God" (1 John 5:20), and the "true witness" (Revelation 3:14). "Gardener" is found only twice in the Bible. It refers to God the Father (John 15:1), and to Jesus when Mary thought He was the gardener (John 20:15).

What does a gardener do? First, let's start with the goal: to produce healthy plants that produce high-quality fruit. To gather a great harvest, a gardener does many things, including preparing the soil, planting, watering, fertilizing, and pruning. There are, of course, many variables, including the weather and soil conditions. Gardening takes a lot of planning, hard work, and time. A good gardener enjoys these tasks because of the end result—a bountiful harvest.

God has the same goal, but His fruit is people. Jesus gives the analogy of a vine because His immediate listeners were familiar with vineyards. But the vineyard Christ refers to is the world, and He is the true Vine who produces fruit that pleases the Father. All other vines are of the world and produce bad fruit—namely people who trust in themselves or other gods. God does everything possible to harvest a bountiful crop of people who will honor Him and live with Him forever.

Jesus is the true Vine, and we are the branches (John 15:5). So how can a branch bear lots of fruit to please the Father? By abiding in the Vine—a minute by minute union with Jesus. The Vine gives life and nutrients to the branches (verses 4-5). Because we're still in this world and imperfect, we need cultivating and pruning to get rid of growths that displease the Father. We want to bear lots of good fruit to honor Him (verses 2-3,8).

Don't despise the pruning process. Thank the Father for loving you so much that He wants you to bear a great harvest.

Question for Today: Are you abiding in the True Vine? Is your life bearing good fruit?

Prayer: Jesus, You are the True Vine, and I want to abide in You all the time. Prune away anything in my life that displeases You so that I can bear even more fruit.

Advocate
Someone Who Always Stands Up for You

*[Jesus said,] "When the Advocate comes, whom I will send
to you from the Father—the Spirit of truth who goes out
from the Father—he will testify about me" (John 15:26).*

FYI: For three years the disciples followed Jesus. They were His closest friends. As the opposition from the Jewish religious leaders intensified, Jesus began telling His twelve disciples that He would soon be
leaving them. They felt abandoned and fearful. Confusion filled their
hearts. But Jesus promised them the greatest gift—the Holy Spirit
who would live inside them. And because each Person of the Trinity
is one with the others, the Triune God who created the world would
live inside them every day of their lives (John 7:37-39; 16:1-15).

Goodbyes with someone you deeply love are difficult…often tearful…often filled with sadness. They are especially hard when you don't
know if you'll see the person soon or never again. When Jesus told His
disciples He was leaving, they were upset. The Messiah, their teacher and
closest friend, was leaving them. How would they get by without Him?
Maybe you've felt similar feelings? If one of your parents has died, you
may feel you no longer have a fatherly or motherly guide in your life. If a
loved one, such as a spouse, sister, or brother has died, you may feel that
you've lost a part of your own life. Maybe your best friend is serving over-
seas for several years at a time. He or she may still be living, but the loss
you feel is deep.

Jesus promised that He wouldn't leave us alone to fight for God's truth
against the world forces. He would send from the Father the Advocate—
the Holy Spirit. An advocate is one who helps, defends, and comforts. The
Holy Spirit gives us courage to stand for truth against all antagonists. The
Spirit is so close to us so He can teach us all the Father wants us to know
and guide us to following God's truth.

The Holy Spirit is the divine indweller of believers in Jesus Christ.
When you feel alone or don't know what to do, the Advocate can fill the
void or guide you to the right choices on thinking and behaving…if you
ask for His help. In times of emotional hurt, He will comfort you. If you

cry out for help, He is there inside you to provide what you need. Jesus said, "Very truly I tell you, it is for your good that I am going away. Unless I go away, the Advocate will not come to you; but if I go, I will send him to you" (John 16:7).

Question for Today: How are you responding to your personal Advocate?

Prayer: Holy Spirit, You are my Advocate as I go through life. Give me Your wise guidance. Let me experience Your divine comfort today.

Spirit of Truth
Deeper into Truth

*[Jesus said,] "When he, the Spirit of truth, comes, he
will guide you into all truth. He will not speak on
his own; he will speak only what he hears, and he
will tell you what is yet to come" (John 16:13).*

FYI: "Spirit of Truth" is also found in John 14:17; 15:26; and 1 John 4:6.
The word "truth" appears 110 times in the New Testament. To find out
more about truth, read John 3:20-21; 4:23-24; 8:31-32; Romans 1:18-20;
15:8; 1 Corinthians 13:6.

It's no fun to believe what someone tells you and then find out it was a lie.
You feel deceived and misled.

But knowing you've heard the truth produces peace because there is
no fear of being deceived. Honesty cuts through deceitfulness, facades,
and cover-ups. Standing on the foundation of truth gives us confidence.
The Spirit of truth emanates from the source of all truth, Jesus Christ. The
Bible says, "The Word became flesh and made his dwelling among us. We
have seen his glory, the glory of the One and Only, who came from the
Father, full of grace and truth" (John 1:14). Pontius Pilate asked Jesus the
ageless question, "What is truth?" (John 18:38). What he didn't realize was
that he was looking at the Source of all truth.

The job of the Spirit of truth is to reveal the truth about Christ to His
followers. The Holy Spirit will lead you deeper into everything you can
grasp about the truth. He won't tell you lies because He is holy and righteous. As you read the Scriptures, which He inspired, ask Him to open
your mind and heart to all He wants you to know and experience.

Question for Today: Are you studying the Bible so the Spirit of truth will
guide you into all truth?

Prayer: Lord, there's so much wrong information in the world. Spirit of
truth, guide me to as much of the truth as You want me to know. I want
to learn more about You. I want to experience You daily.

Only True God
The Real Definition of Eternal Life

*[Jesus prayed,] "This is eternal life: that they
may know you, the only true God, and Jesus
Christ, whom you have sent" (John 17:3).*

FYI: This is the only time in the Bible that the name "only true God" is
given. Jesus Christ's definition of "eternal life" isn't endless existence.
Rather, it's a close, personal relationship with God and Christ. One
of Jesus' prayers shortly before His arrest and death is recorded in
John 17.

The most famous portrait in the world is the *Mona Lisa*, circa 1506, by Italian artist Leonardo da Vinci. To see it, you don't have to visit the Louvre Museum in Paris where it's on permanent on display. Reproductions have been made of the painting, and it's been copied thousands of times. You can even get an iPhone cover or kitchen towel decorated with the image. To commemorate Leonardo's five hundredth birthday, an image of the *Mona Lisa* was printed on a West German postage stamp in 1952. The original *Mona Lisa* is priceless and treasured. All the reproductions, copies, prints, and duplications are cheap by comparison. An original is always more valuable than the imitation.

When it comes to God, He's not even in the same category as something created by a human being. God is the only true God. Nothing comes close to Him. All other gods and substitutes people worship are pathetic forgeries. Since the "only true God" is eternal, He is the only One who can define eternal life. There have been thousands of people throughout the millennia who have attempted to describe the afterlife. Movies, books, paintings, and various religious organizations have tried to depict heaven and how to get there. None of them is correct because none have actually been there. It's like trying to describe the ocean and the creatures that live there when you've always lived in the desert.

There are myriads of theories on how to get eternal life espoused by religious leaders, laypeople, and even charlatans. But they all conjure up cheap imitations at best. There is only one authentic way to eternal life—to know the only true God through His Son, Jesus Christ. He reveals God to us.

The only true God is eternal, and He sent His one and only Son to tell us what heaven is like and how to get there. The entire Bible presents God's plan to bring people back to Himself.

Question for Today: Do you have eternal life? How do you know?

Prayer: You are the only true God, and the only One who can give me eternal life. Your way is right and perfect because You are perfect. Fill my entire being with You.

Holy Father
I Am Coming Home

[Jesus prayed,] "I will remain in the world no longer, but they are still in the world, and I am coming to you. Holy Father, protect them by the power of your name, the name you gave me, so that they may be one as we are one" (John 17:11).

FYI: This is the only time in the Bible that God is called "holy Father." In this farewell prayer, Jesus tenderly calls God "Father" (John 17:1,5,21,24). It reveals a close intimacy and absolute trust. Jesus also called Him "righteous Father" (verse 25). God is the only perfect Father!

"Mom and Dad, I'm finally coming home." Statements like that from adult children after a long time away from a loving family reveal a tender spot in their hearts. When we return from school, service, living in another state, or visiting a different country, our hearts yearn to reconnect with familiar people and see familiar places again. It will be so good to see our families again and to catch up on all that has happened while we were away.

But leaving to head home is bittersweet. We'll miss all the new friends we've acquired while we were away. We promise our buddies we will keep in contact. Though it's hard to leave, the emotional pull to go back home is strong.

If you've felt these kinds of emotions, imagine how Jesus felt about going back to His Father. The deeply personal and passionate prayer of Jesus the night before He was crucified reveals these same feelings. Less than twenty-four hours later, He would be dead—crucified on a cross for you and me. Only thirty-three years earlier, Jesus, in a sense, had to say goodbye to His Father in heaven to come to earth to redeem us from the power of Satan. Now He is saying farewell to His closest disciples. They would no longer have His physical presence as they faced the daunting task of spreading His message of love and salvation throughout the world.

Jesus was facing a horrible death, and His disciples would scatter and be frightened. Praying that the holy Father would protect the people He fervently loved, Jesus knew His Father intimately and trusted Him infinitely. Jesus knew the Father would be true to His character, as revealed in His names, including *Jehovah*, the Almighty, *Elohim*, Creator, and so many others.

For what purpose did Jesus want His disciples empowered by His heavenly Father? To mold their hearts together so they would love each other just like He and His holy Father love each other. As Jesus was going to His death and then home to heaven, He had on His heart and in His prayer His disciples and all those who would become His followers throughout history.

Question for Today: Why do you think Jesus wanted His followers to be united by His holy Father?

Prayer: Holy Father, thank You for loving me so much. Fill me with Your power to love those You put in my path. Mold our hearts together so we can serve You better.

Righteous Father
Become Like the Best

*[Jesus prayed,] "Righteous Father, though the
world does not know you, I know you, and they
know that you have sent me" (John 17:25).*

FYI: Jesus clearly stated that the Father loved Him (John 3:35; 5:20;
10:17). Jesus showed His great love for His Father by obeying Him
(John 5:19,36; 8:28), showing His great works (John 10:25,32), honoring Him (John 8:49), and entrusting His spirit to Him (Luke 23:46).

Fathers have a profound and lasting influence on their children. If your dad was emotionally distant, you may feel that God is also distant. If your dad was abusive or harsh, you may believe God is often angry at you too. You can either be thankful for your father's input into your life or rebel against his influence. Your father can build either good or bad traits into you. Either way, he's influenced your attitudes, habits, and behaviors.

How did Jesus feel about His Father? Jesus called His Father righteous, meaning He had no faults, no imperfections. He does everything totally right all the time. No earthly father can reach that height of perfection. Jesus knew His Father perfectly for all eternity, and He chose to reveal His Father to His disciples. His deepest desire was for His followers to know the Father also (John 17:3).

The influence of the righteous Father on His Son was so profound that Jesus brought Him glory by finishing the work the Father had sent Him to do and glorifying His Father (John 17:4-5,22; 12:28,50). He revealed to His followers as much of the Father as the human mind can comprehend.

Do you want to know what God the Father is like? Learn what Jesus revealed about Him. Jesus said, "Anyone who has seen me has seen the Father" (John 14:9). Focus on the righteous Father and pray to become more like Him.

Question for Today: What is your relationship with the righteous Father?

Prayer: Righteous Father, You are the perfect Parent. No earthly father compares to You. Influence my life and impact my whole being with Your righteousness and goodness.

Rabbi
Kiss of Death

Going at once to Jesus, Judas said, "Rabbi!"
and kissed him (Mark 14:45).

FYI: People addressed Jesus as "Rabbi" twelve other times in God's Word. In all cases they were showing genuine respect and honor, unlike in today's verse. After his betrayal of Jesus, Judas gave back the money he'd been paid and committed suicide (Matthew 27:3-5).

"Kiss of death." You may have heard the expression. It means something that is ultimately a disaster, a tragedy, or a total failure. The outcome is destined to be calamitous...even fatal. You may have said something like, "This bad grade in chemistry is the kiss of death to my going to medical school" or "When my fiancé told me we were just not meant for each other, I realized it was the kiss of death to our future marriage." The phrase has been used in movies, songs, poetry, and books. During the Cold War, the Russian KGB created a spy pistol called "Kiss of Death" because it looked like a tube of lipstick and could shoot one bullet. In the world of the mafia, when a mob boss kisses someone on the cheek, it signifies that the person is going to be killed.

So what is the origin of the phrase "kiss of death"? The Bible. Here's the scene.

Jesus and the disciples were together for the Passover meal. At some point, Judas left to betray Jesus. The disciple had collaborated with the religious leaders to capture Jesus. They wanted to get Him as soon as possible, and because it was Passover, most of the Jews would be at home. The leaders wanted the arrest and trial done quietly to avoid a scene and because they were breaking Jewish law (to hold the trial at that time). The Jewish leaders arranged for thugs with clubs and swords to accompany Judas to the garden of Gethsemane, on the outskirts of Jerusalem. That's where Jesus would be. Judas told his mob, "The one I kiss is the man; arrest him and lead him away under guard" (Mark 14:44).

Approaching his former friend, Judas addressed Jesus as "Rabbi," which means teacher and is usually an honorable form of address. Coming from the lips of Judas, however, it was cold and deceitful. It wasn't an honored greeting, but a signal for the armed mob to grab Him.

Judas had been a disciple of Jesus for more than two years. As a disciple, he'd heard the teachings of Jesus and witnessed many miracles. He'd heard people call Jesus "Lord," "Christ," "Chosen One," "Holy One of God," "Son of God," "Son of Man," and other titles of respect and honor. Judas rejected them all. With a black heart, he kissed Jesus as an act of betrayal and condemnation.

Question for Today: Why do you think Judas betrayed Jesus after having followed Him for two years?

Prayer: Rabbi, You are the greatest teacher who ever walked on the earth. Unfortunately, I too have denied You at times and turned my back on You and Your teachings. Please forgive me and draw me closer to You.

Son of the Blessed One
Freedom or the Cross?

Jesus remained silent and gave no answer. Again
the high priest asked him, "Are you the Messiah, the
Son of the Blessed One?" (Mark 14:61).

FYI: This is the only time "Son of the Blessed One" appears. Nowhere else is God called "the Blessed One." The person referring to Jesus and God isn't honoring either one of them.

When parents angrily shout, "Did you do this?" while pointing to a broken glass, the child in front of them cringes. The way the question was asked told the child it wasn't to gain information but to make an accusation. The "board of education" might soon be applied to the child's "seat of learning." Bosses can ask accusing questions. So can your spouse and neighbors. When that happens, you usually know that, no matter what your answer will be, you'll be deemed guilty.

Jesus was asked an accusing question—not for something He did wrong, but to give His accusers justification for demanding His death. Only the Romans, who were ruling Israel at the time, had the authority and power to sentence a guilty party to death and carry out capital punishment. For the Jewish religious leaders to convince the Roman governor to execute Jesus, they had to obtain evidence that He was a dangerous criminal. The only charge they could convict Him of was blasphemy (a human being claiming to be God). His captors took Jesus to the chief priest. Other Jewish priests and leaders were gathered there as well (Mark 14:53-59).

Much to their despair, these belligerent accusers couldn't find anything against Jesus that would stick. Their case was quickly disintegrating. In desperation, the chief priest asked the accusing question: "Are you the Messiah, the Son of the Blessed One?"

Jesus shot back, "Yes, I am." And to make sure they understood what He was saying, He confidently added that they would see "the Son of Man sitting at the right hand of the Mighty One" (Mark 14:62).

Jesus could have answered "No" to their accusations, and they might have had to let Him go free at that point. But He chose to tell the truth, incriminating Himself by clearly making Himself equal to God. His accusers then condemned Him.

Jesus Christ, the Son of the Blessed One, chose death on the cross to give us the freedom to approach God. Praise His holy name!

Question for Today: In front of accusers, how would you answer a similar question about your faith? "Do you really think Jesus is God?"

Prayer: Son of the Blessed One, thank You for telling the truth when You knew it would cost You Your life. You didn't cringe or tell a lie to save Yourself. I am eternally grateful for Your boldness. Help me proclaim Your deity today.

Chosen One
Choosing to Wait

*The people stood watching, and the rulers even sneered at
him. They said, "He saved others; let him save himself if
he is God's Messiah, the Chosen One" (Luke 23:35).*

FYI: The name "Chosen One" in reference to Jesus only appears one
other time in the New Testament. John the Baptist was Jesus' cousin,
but he testified that he didn't realize Jesus was the Chosen One until
the Holy Spirit descended on Him (John 1:32-34).

Transport yourself back to middle school. You're sitting in class, and the
teacher asks a question. There's a student in your class who has the right
answer. In fact, it seems like he often has the right answer. Perhaps that
student was you. Or maybe it was someone you envied, especially because
the teacher appreciated that student. That student seemed to have a special relationship with the teacher. In your anger and frustration, you may
have called that student "teacher's pet."

Something similar was going on when Jesus hung on the cross. The
bystanders sneered at Him and called Him names. They knew Jesus
claimed to be God's Son—the Messiah, the Chosen One. They turned
His special name into an insult. They knew Jesus had a close relationship
with God. They assumed that if God really loved this man, He would
intervene. If Jesus really was the Chosen One, then surely He could get
Himself down from the cross. Surely, the Son of God could save Himself.

But in this passage—as in many others throughout the Gospels—
Jesus doesn't act as people expected Him to. The King of kings who was
born in the filth of a barn wouldn't get down off the cross in response to
the jeers of the people. Being the Chosen One didn't mean living without pain, trials, and suffering. Being the Chosen One didn't mean being
dependent on human expectations and schedules.

Despite the scorn, the Chosen One did something better for the people than get down from the cross. He submitted to death and then rose
from the grave. He proved—in God's timing, not ours—that God had
not abandoned Him. He proved He was the Savior of the world; He was

the One whom God had chosen to defeat death and usher in new life for humanity.

Question for Today: Reflect on the last time you questioned whether the Chosen One would fulfill His promises to you. How did He work differently than you expected?

Prayer: Dear Chosen One, You are the Messiah! God selected You to defeat death and give me everlasting life. Thank You for showing me that You work in ways I can't regulate. Thank You for staying dependent on Your Father. Help me wait patiently instead of getting angry when I can't see how You are working in my situation.

Rabboni
One Word Changes the Picture

Jesus said to her, "Mary." She turned toward him and cried out in Aramaic, "Rabboni!" (which means "Teacher") (John 20:16).

FYI: *Rabboni* is an unusual way to address someone. It's more of a title than a word of greeting. It's a form of the word *rabbi*, meaning "teacher," but it implies much more respect and dignity.

There may be one or two people in your life who have keys to your heart. Probably over the years, you've progressively opened more of your life and soul to them. When you talk on the phone, just the sound of their voices can thrill your heart. The very first words they speak capture your attention. "Honey" from your sweetheart sounds so warm and caring. When your toddler chirps "Dad" or "Mom," your heart skips a beat. You respond immediately when the phone rings because you're expecting a call from someone you love. You know the sensation. You feel like melted butter inside.

Can you imagine how Mary Magdalene felt when she heard her name spoken by the risen Savior? What an emotional day! Mary and some other women went to the tomb, but when they arrived it was empty. "Suddenly two men in clothes that gleamed like lightning stood beside them." They announced that Jesus was risen (Luke 24:4-7). The women ran to tell the disciples (Matthew 28:8), and then Peter and John rushed to the tomb (John 20:3-8).

After the two disciples left, Mary was by herself. She looks into the tomb again, and two angels ask her why she's crying. She replies, "They have taken my Lord away...and I don't know where they have put Him" (John 20:13). Distraught and tearful, she turns and sees a man who asks her, "Woman, why are you crying?" She didn't recognize Him, so she asked, "Sir, if you have carried him away, tell me where you have put him, and I will get him" (verse 15).

As Mary turned to go, Jesus called her name softly and compassionately in a voice she recognized. She instantly turned back to Him. Her heart leaped. *Jesus!* Her depression immediately turned to elation. "Rabboni!" she exclaimed. This tender title means "my great Master."

Mary's name is the first recorded word Jesus spoke after His resurrection. He rewarded her love and devotion by revealing Himself to her first. Jesus will reward your love and devotion also.

Question for Today: Are you listening for Jesus' soft, loving voice in your heart?

Prayer: *Rabboni,* open my heart and senses to You. I want to hear Your soft voice deep in my heart. Teach me more about You. My heart sings Your praises.

Author of Life
Dead...but Raised

*You killed the author of life, but God raised him from
the dead. We are witnesses of this (Acts 3:15).*

FYI: This is the only time the name "author of life" is given. The New
Testament states 47 times that God raised Jesus from the dead, and
it predicts Jesus will rise from the dead 9 times. Only once does it say
that Christ raised Himself, but that was referring to the Jewish temple as a veiled analogy to His body (John 2:19).

After a famous speaker finishes addressing a crowd, people often line up
to purchase the speaker's book and get his or her autograph. Some authors
only write; they aren't professional speakers. People still like to get their
autographs. A book that has the writer's signature inside is considered
more valuable.

The idea of "author" has many more applications than writing a book.
The title "author" means "the originator, the source, the starter of something new." Authors bring into existence that which didn't exist before.

Who did the crazed crowd want killed that dark day of the crucifixion?
What did they shout at the top of their lungs for Pilate to do with "Jesus
who is called the Messiah"? "Crucify Him!" They rejected Pilate's offer to
grant mercy to Jesus and have the murderer Barabbas executed instead
of Jesus of Nazareth. But the crowd shouted even more for Jesus' death.

In their hatred, and hostility, and mob mentality, they voted to crucify the Author of life. The very One who gave them life and created the
entire universe: "Through [Jesus Christ] all things were made; without
him nothing was made that has been made. In him was life, and that life
was the light of all mankind" (John 1:3-4).

And now Peter was boldly speaking directly to the supporters of killing Jesus Christ. Peter said, "You killed the author of life, but God raised
him from the dead." The angry mob had done its evil, but God stepped in
and raised Jesus Christ from the grave. The One who willingly laid down
His life, God picked up. Peter told the people that they'd seen Him, talked
with Him, eaten with Him. And now he was proclaiming that the Author
of life was raised from the dead. Jesus was alive! "Repent, then, and turn

to God, so that your sins may be wiped out, that times of refreshing may come from the Lord, and that he may send the Messiah, who has been appointed for you—even Jesus" (Acts 3:19-20).

The crowd who shouted "crucify him" that day represents all of us. If we'd been there, we probably would have shouted for Jesus' death too. I believe we are just as guilty of the murder of the Author of life as they were.

Question for Today: Have you repented from your sins that Jesus died to erase from God's sight?

Prayer: I'm deeply humbled, Author of life, because my sins and selfishness are what You died for on the cross. You are the Author of my salvation. I repent of my sins and ask for your forgiveness.

Prince
Bold Obedience

*God exalted him to his own right hand as
Prince and Savior that he might bring Israel to
repentance and forgive their sins (Acts 5:31).*

FYI: The word "prince" means one who has royal dignity, authority, and power. Read Isaiah 9:6 and Daniel 8:23-25 to see their connection with Acts 5:31.

When we do something right, we expect those affected to say thanks. We're completely surprised when we receive negative blowback or are accused of doing something wrong. We've all heard news stories about whistleblowers who exposed misconduct or corruption in an organization and were subsequently demoted or fired by clever bosses outmaneuvering the law.

There is a similar news story that happened to Nehemiah. He was exiled in Persia, a thousand miles away from Jerusalem. He heard about the plight of the Jewish people in that city after much of it had been destroyed in 586 BC. He asked the king he served to allow him to go back and take supplies to rebuild the protective wall around the city. The king agreed.

The officials of the surrounding nations reacted angrily to Nehemiah's plans. "When Sanballat the Horonite and Tobiah the Ammonite official heard about this, they were very much disturbed that someone had come to promote the welfare of the Israelites" (Nehemiah 2:10). More than 600 years later, a similar situation engulfed Jerusalem. After Pentecost, the day when the Holy Spirit filled the disciples, they performed many miracles and spoke to the crowds about the crucifixion and resurrection of Jesus Christ (Acts 2:1-4,10). Many people enthusiastically responded by seeking forgiveness for crucifying Jesus and accepting Him as their Savior. However, the religious leaders reacted angrily to the apostles' teachings. "They called [Peter and John] in again and commanded them not to speak or teach at all in the name of Jesus" (Acts 4:18).

The apostles defied "the establishment" and kept proclaiming the gospel—the "good news" of Jesus Christ. They were jailed, hauled before the Sanhedrin, and reprimanded. Peter boldly said, "We must obey God rather than human beings! The God of our ancestors raised Jesus from the dead—whom you killed by hanging him on a cross" (Acts 5:29-30). God exalted Jesus as Prince. That meant that the humble man they had crucified became the ruler of the world.

Question for Today: If you were confronted by authorities and told not to talk about Jesus or share the gospel, what would you do?

Prayer: My whole body and soul bow down before You and worship You, my Prince and Savior. Regardless of what others say, I'm determined to follow and obey You.

Seed
A Promise Fulfilled

Why, then, was the law given at all? It was added because
of transgressions until the Seed to whom the promise
referred had come. The law was given through angels
and entrusted to a mediator (Galatians 3:19).

FYI: The word "seed" occurs 89 times in the Bible, but this is the only time it's used as a name of God. A further explanation for the Son of God appearing is found in 1 John 3:8-9.

When you entered high school you wanted to graduate, but it took four years to accomplish that. If you entered college, you may have said you wanted to be a doctor, own your own business, become a teacher, or enter some other profession. It took many years to finally reach your goal.

After Adam and Eve sinned, God put a curse on Satan, the deceiver who was disguised as a snake. The Lord said to Satan, "I will put enmity between you and the woman, and between your offspring and hers; he will crush your head, and you will strike his heel" (Genesis 3:15). It took thousands of years to realize the fulfillment of that statement. The word "offspring" is a translation of the Hebrew word for "seed." The Seed of the woman would crush the head of the seed of Satan, although the seed of Satan would strike His heel. This is what took place on the cross. The followers of Satan crucified the offspring of the virgin Mary and thought they'd won when Jesus died. That was on a Friday.

On Sunday, God raised the Seed of the woman out of the grave, fulfilling His promise. Christ's resurrection defeated death and guaranteed the ultimate destruction of Satan and his followers (Revelation 20:10-15). The law given to Moses showed that people could not keep it perfectly. People naturally sin against God. The Seed, Jesus, offers salvation from the penalty of transgressing the law. Praise be to God and the Seed forever!

Question for Today: From whose seed are you?

Prayer: Oh Seed, thank You for fulfilling God's promise and saving me from Satan's domination.

Spirit of His Son
From Enemies to Family Members

Because you are his sons, God sent the Spirit of his Son into our hearts, the Spirit who calls out, "Abba, Father" (Galatians 4:6).

FYI: This is the only occurrence of the "Spirit of His Son" in the Bible. Read again the other verses where the word *Abba* is found (Mark 14:36; Romans 8:15). Each verse has the Aramaic word *Abba* followed by the Greek word translated "Father." Why do you think an Aramaic word is connected to a Greek word?

Wanting to belong is one of our deepest desires. When we're part of a group that has shared interests and an affinity for each other, strong personal bonds develop. The most significant bonds are formed when we become children of God through trusting Christ as our Savior. Even though we may have vastly different backgrounds, languages, and cultures, what unites us is our relationship with Jesus. When we receive Christ into our hearts, we're born again through the work of the Spirit (John 3:5-8). Before this event, we're *creations* of God but not *children* of God. We become children of God when we believe in Christ. The unifying factor is the indwelling "Spirit of his Son." He cleanses us of our sin, and we're adopted into God's family for eternity.

Before we gave our lives to Christ, God was our enemy (Romans 5:8-11). Now, the Spirit of His Son has entered our hearts, so we can call God *"Abba,* Father." *Abba* is the Aramaic word for "daddy." Along with millions of other Christians throughout the world, living and dead, we belong in His family. The Father wants us to build strong relationships with other believers; thus, our need for belonging is solved.

Question for Today: How is the Spirit of God's Son working in your heart?

Prayer: How wonderful to belong in Your awesome family. Spirit of His Son, thank You for making a close relationship with my heavenly Daddy possible.

Spirit of Jesus
Detour to a Better Destination

When they came to the border of Mysia, they
tried to enter Bithynia, but the Spirit of Jesus
would not allow them to (Acts 16:7).

FYI: Mysia and Bithynia were regions (now northwest and north Turkey) that the Romans had conquered and annexed into part of Asia Minor. The Roman Empire extended around the Mediterranean and through modern-day Europe. Europe became the most powerful area of the world for many centuries. The Europeans spread their influence worldwide, taking the gospel with them. Christianity spread like wildfire, transforming millions of people through the power of salvation through the life, death, and resurrection of Jesus.

Paul was on his second missionary journey in the western part of Asia Minor. He planned to head toward the northwest, but the Spirit of Jesus intervened, essentially saying, "I have a different destination for you." So Paul traveled west to the seaport city of Troas, where God gave him a vision to spread the gospel to Macedonia and Europe (Acts 16:8-10). Because the gospel writings were in Greek, the common language at the time, and the Roman Empire brought peace to the entire region, the messages of Jesus spread quickly. Over the following centuries, as people became more mobile, the gospel spread around the world. If Paul had gone eastward into Asia as he'd planned, the gospel might not have spread so quickly. Even though God doesn't always answer our "Why?" questions, we can trust Him to lead us where He wants us. His plans are beyond what our finite minds can grasp.

Question for Today: When has God changed the direction you were headed? How did you feel about it at the time?

Prayer: Spirit of Jesus, I totally submit to Your leadership. As I humble myself to do God's will, show me the road You want me to take. Wherever You lead, I will gladly follow and obey.

Lord of Peace
All Types of People

May the Lord of peace himself give you peace at all times and in every way. The Lord be with all of you (2 Thessalonians 3:16).

FYI: This is the only place in the Bible that God is called the "Lord of peace." The Thessalonian believers were facing severe problems, and some had died. At times their newfound faith was shaky as they struggled with living their faith. Paul assured them that their faith in the Lord, who has everything in His hands, would bring peace even if some of their questions weren't totally resolved.

People are strange, aren't they? A person you love can repeatedly break your heart. Someone at work, in church, or in your neighborhood may upset you. Others who love you never give you any problems. It can be confusing as we strive to maintain healthy relationships and avoid destructive ones.

It would be great if there was a book of guidelines to give us discernment between good and bad relationships. Well, there is such a book—the Bible! Paul tells the Christians at Thessalonica to encourage the people who really wanted to follow Christ and to reprove those who were behaving badly. That advice applies to us today, as well. To do that, we need to develop discernment, wisdom, courage, sensitivity, patience, and honesty.

Remember, God is faithful, and He will strengthen and protect us from the evil one. That alone can bring peace to our hearts. There is Someone looking out for us! We are not left alone to try to figure things out.

To stand strong and continue following the way of the Lord of peace, we must persevere. As humans, we are fallible and prone to doubt and fear. The way to overcome these feelings is to continue submitting ourselves to the Lord, who will give us peace "at all times and in every way." Knowing that will bring clarity in the midst of confusing relationships.

Question for Today: What keeps you from trusting the Lord of peace at all times and in every way?

Prayer: Lord of peace, I ask You to take hold of my entire life. Protect me and strengthen me so that I will persevere and trust You today...and every day.

Lord of Glory
Jesus' Trials Were Illegal

None of the rulers of this age understood it, for if they had, they would not have crucified the Lord of glory (1 Corinthians 2:8).

FYI: "Lord of glory" is used only one time in the Bible. "Glory" is synonymous with "heaven" (1 Timothy 3:16). Jesus possesses heaven's majesty.

Educated and highly intellectual individuals can be wrong. Look at some of the foolish personal and financial decisions some of them make. Leaders of businesses, universities, and governments frequently make wrong choices. They make decisions based on the information at hand, but they still aren't always right.

People can have lots of education, knowledge, and authority, but still possess very little wisdom. They can be so smart and, at the same time, so blind. The history of civilization displays the rise and fall of rulers, generals, and sages who made wrong choices and unwise decisions. The leaders of Israel and Rome chose to crucify Jesus. That was the most foolish decision in all of history! There is the wisdom of the age, and there is the wisdom of God. They are often antithetical to each other (1 Corinthians 2:6-7). The six trials of Jesus reveal how the Jewish and Roman officials made such flawed decisions that led to the worst one of all.

Trial 1. Annas, the powerful Jewish high priest emeritus, asked Jesus questions as if interested in His answers but allowed an officer to slug Him (John 18:19-22).

Trial 2. Caiaphas, the current Jewish high priest, asked, "Are You the Messiah, the Son of the Blessed One?" then allowed the people present to beat Him (Mark 14:61-65).

Trial 3. The council of the elders of the people (the Sanhedrin), comprised of the seventy top Jewish religious leaders, refused to believe Jesus (Luke 22:66-71).

Trial 4. Pilate, the Roman governor, found no fault in Jesus, but gave in to Jesus' accusers and sent Him to Herod (Luke 23:4-7).

Trial 5. Herod Antipas treated Jesus with contempt and then sent Him back to Pilate (Luke 23:11).

Trial 6. Pilate knew Jesus was innocent, but the governor succumbed to mob pressure and granted their request to condemn and murder Jesus (Luke 23:23-25).

These highly educated leaders were face-to-face with the Lord of glory and treated Him like a heinous murderer. Jesus' trials before the Jewish leaders broke their laws of trial procedures. The judges were His prosecutors, and they knowingly accepted false testimonies. They allowed the jurors and officers to mock Jesus, spit on Him, beat Him, and torture Him right in the courtroom. And then they encouraged the riotous mob to support their cause! The leaders knew Jesus was innocent, but they condemned Him. Both Jews and Gentiles were guilty of His death. The world crucified the Lord of glory.

Question for Today: What role does your sin play in the suffering and death of Jesus?

Prayer: Lord, You were the magnificent God who came into our environment, and yet we murdered You. O Lord of glory, You forgive the guilty ones who humbly turn to You. I'm forgiven! I praise You.

Spirit of Our God
God's Bar of Soap

Wrongdoers...that is what some of you were. But you were washed, you were sanctified, you were justified in the name of the Lord Jesus Christ and by the Spirit of our God (1 Corinthians 6:9,11).

FYI: Only this verse contains the name "Spirit of our God." The Holy Spirit gives spiritual birth to believers (John 3:5-8). You can read more about "washing" in Ephesians 5:26; Titus 3:5; Hebrews 10:22; James 4:8; Revelation 7:14; 22:14.

Soap and water do wonders for our dirty hands and bodies. After using them, we feel clean and refreshed. But what can we use to clean up when we know our soul is full of filth and sin? There are no soul cleansers on supermarket shelves. First Corinthians 6:9 says wrongdoers won't inherit the kingdom of God. But when we confess our sins to Christ and put our faith in Him, we're transferred from the kingdom of darkness to the kingdom of light (Colossians 1:12-13). And this soul cleanser is offered free of charge by Jesus Christ when He willingly shed His blood for you and me.

When we trust in Christ for salvation, the Spirit of our God washes our sins away, cleanses (sanctifies) us, and justifies us—making us righteous before God. We're set free from sin and welcomed into God's family. Amazing!

Question for Today: From what have you been washed, sanctified, and justified?

Prayer: My soul will rejoice forever, Spirit of our God. You've made me righteous. Thank You, Jesus, for shedding Your blood so that I can have right standing before God.

Last Adam
Which Adam Is Your Leader?

It is written: "The first man Adam became a living being";
the last Adam, a life-giving spirit (1 Corinthians 15:45).

FYI: Eve sinned first because she was deceived by the serpent (Genesis 3:1-6). Adam wasn't deceived, so he had a clear choice: to give in to Eve's offer of the fruit or to reject it and obey God. He chose to reject God (Genesis 3:6; 1 Timothy 2:14). I'm sure they would have loved to have a "reset" button.

When working with computers, we sometimes hit a snag and the program "freezes." Nothing on the screen works. Game consoles have a similar problem. The solution? They have reset buttons! Pressing this button clears the memory and reboots the device.

Wouldn't it be great to have a "life reset" button? Fiction writers have come up with all sorts of time machines to go back in time to relive and alter certain events. That way the characters in the plot can do something different this time around and change the results. Imagine what it would be like if you got a bad grade on a final exam. You'd just have to push the reset button and retake the exam. Or suppose you're in a job that frustrates you? Just push the reset button and you're in a different job. If you were in a car accident, just push the reset button and take a different road.

That sounds fabulous for a fantasy world, but there is no such button in real life *except* for the "last Adam." Only two perfect men have ever walked on this earth—Adam and Christ. Both could have lived forever. Both were tempted by Satan to rebel against God. Adam lived in a perfect environment with everything going his way. God commanded him, "You are free to eat from any tree in the garden; but you must not eat from the tree of the knowledge of good and evil, for when you eat from it you will certainly die" (Genesis 2:16-17). Satan tempted Adam and he listened and chose to disobey God, resulting in all his descendants being born under the curse of physical and spiritual death.

But the "last Adam"—Jesus Christ—was totally different. He lived in a fallen world with everything going against Him. Satan tempted Him, and yet Jesus chose to obey God. Our Savior didn't have to die, but He chose to die for our sins, resulting in eternal life for all who put their faith in Him. "In Adam all die, so in Christ all will be made alive. But each in turn: Christ, the firstfruits; then, when he comes, those who belong to him" (1 Corinthians 15:22-23). Adam's choices brought death. Jesus' choices brought life. Jesus is our reset button.

Question for Today: Which Adam do you follow—the first one or the last One?

Prayer: Oh Jesus, You are the last Adam. You gave me the opportunity to reset my life from a destiny of death to a destiny of life. I choose to follow You!

Father of Compassion
The Person Who Gives Comfort

*Praise be to the God and Father of our Lord
Jesus Christ, the Father of compassion and the
God of all comfort (2 Corinthians 1:3).*

FYI: These two unique names of God appear only in this verse. God initiated compassion and is the embodiment of comfort. True and lasting support and encouragement come only from Him.

The brokenness of the world in which we live is inescapable. Deep grief, heartache, loss, rejection, and abandonment are common to all of us. At times, we feel unloved, unwanted, and unimportant. At such times we need to run to Someone who will understand and provide comfort. We're like an injured child running into a parent's arms…into Your arms, God. You are the deepest source of love, kindness, and empathy. You offer comfort during *all* our troubles.

There is a purpose in God's comfort. The support and hope He gives us is to overflow into the lives of the people we reach out to during their times of trouble. We can do this because the comfort we experience is not our own. We've received it from the Father of compassion. We can thank Him for the comfort He gives us even as we look for opportunities to pass on that comfort to others who need it.

Question for Today: No matter how big or how small, how do you need God's comfort today?

Prayer: Father of compassion, thank You for Your comfort. Lead me to reach out to others who are hurting.

Spirit of the Living God
Success in God's Eyes

You show that you are a letter from Christ, the result
of our ministry, written not with ink but with the
Spirit of the living God, not on tablets of stone but
on tablets of human hearts (2 Corinthians 3:3).

FYI: This is the only time in the Bible that the name "Spirit of the Living God" is used. Paul was traveling widely and preaching about Jesus. But there were false teachers spreading lies about him. They came to Corinth with false letters of recommendation so the Corinthians would believe they were qualified to teach new doctrine.

Success is difficult to define and attain. Who decides when we're successful? Our company may give us an achievement award. We could have just graduated with an advanced educational degree. Perhaps our investments are now significant. Are we successful now?

Those are signs of success as defined by the world. But real success is determined by God, not the world. Real success is eternal, worldly success is fleeting. Paul said that his sign of success was the believers in Christ. They were letters of recommendation from Christ. How so? Well, the Spirit of the living God inscribed His identity on the tablets of their hearts. That's a sign of true success—the Spirit of the living God testifying on our behalf.

When we help people come closer to the Lord, we're helping them become letters from Christ to the world. That is real success in God's eyes. Regardless of any worldly success, do God's will at home, at work, or wherever you are and trust the Spirit of the living God to give you the success that lasts forever.

Question for Today: In what endeavors do you feel you're successful? Are those endeavors eternal?

Prayer: Spirit of the living God, please give me the confidence to help others come to Christ.

God of Love and Peace
From Dysfunction to Harmony

*Brothers and sisters, rejoice! Strive for full restoration, encourage
one another, be of one mind, live in peace. And the God of
love and peace will be with you (2 Corinthians 13:11).*

FYI: This is the only time this name is given in the Bible. Some scholars think Paul wrote more than the two letters to the Corinthian church we have in our Bibles. He may have written a "lost" letter before he wrote 1 Corinthians and, perhaps, a letter of uncompromising exhortation before he wrote 2 Corinthians.

The Christian church in Corinth was a troubled one with a variety of problems. There were divisions among the people, and the leaders tolerated sexual immorality (1 Corinthians 3:5). In his second letter, as recorded in the Bible, Paul confronted the people who opposed his teachings and the Jewish troublemakers who came into the church to pull people away from the gospel (2 Corinthians 10–13). So how does he say goodbye after dealing with so many problems? He ends his letter with joy and hope that aren't based on some superficial wish. No, they are based on the presence of the God of love and peace. He is the only One who can bring dysfunctional people together in unity and restore their relationship with Him. That won't be easy, so the people must desire it and strive for it. Harmony comes from humility. Encouragement builds others up and creates a dynamic team spirit: I am for you, and you are for me.

To "be of one mind" doesn't mean that everyone thinks exactly the same. Being of one mind means we appreciate our differences, and we can work together to serve and glorify the Lord. Pride and selfishness destroy harmony, but peace brings friendship and togetherness. The God of love and peace will help us overcome our weaknesses and help us unite through His Son, Jesus Christ. This is the best hope we can give people.

Question for Today: Do you need harmony with someone today? What will you do about it?

Prayer: God of love and peace, fill me today. Help me solve any conflicts and dysfunctions that come up in in my relationships. I want restoration, encouragement, harmony, and peace in Your name.

Spirit of Christ
It Matters Who Is in Control

*You, however, are not in the realm of the flesh but are
in the realm of the Spirit, if indeed the Spirit of God
lives in you. And if anyone does not have the Spirit of
Christ, they do not belong to Christ (Romans 8:9).*

FYI: The name "Spirit of Christ" appears only twice in the Bible—here
and in 1 Peter 1:11. In both passages, the Spirit of Christ points people
to Jesus.

How hard is it for you to give a compliment? It's easier for some than others. It's hardest when we're having a bad day, when we feel lonely or hurt, when we feel nobody understands what we're going through. Sometimes what we really feel like saying is the opposite of a compliment.

But if we do decide to go with a harsh word or an insult, we often regret it later. Sarcasm doesn't affirm or elevate people. Unpleasant statements push people down, and insulting someone is not what the Spirit of Christ is about. He is about elevating Jesus Christ. Without accepting Jesus into our hearts, we live as ordinary people subjected to the whims of our sin nature. Unfortunately, that comes with consequences.

If you make a commitment to Jesus and allow Him into your heart, His Spirit will transform your life and give you the gift of eternal life. The Spirit of Christ actually dwells in your heart. That is the proof that you belong to Christ. As He works in your life, it will become evident to others that there is something different about you. Your attitudes, speech, and behavior will display His presence. You'll be lifting up others and walking in God's ways. What a difference the Spirit of Christ can make!

Question for Today: Can people see that the Spirit of Christ dwells in you?

Prayer: Spirit of Christ, thank You that You dwell in me because I put my faith in You. Transform me so that others will see You in my life and want to know You too.

Abba
Adopted into a Forever Family

The Spirit you received does not make you slaves, so
that you live in fear again; rather, the Spirit you
received brought about your adoption to sonship. And
by him we cry, "Abba, Father" (Romans 8:15).

FYI: In ancient Middle East and Roman times, adoption meant children legally became members of a family other than their families of origin. An adopted child received the family name and was on an equal basis with the biological children. Adoption meant that the child would receive all the benefits and any inheritance just as if he or she had been born into that family. Moses was adopted by Pharaoh's daughter; Esther was adopted by Mordecai (Exodus 2:10; Esther 2:7).

"Adoption." That word conjures up many different attitudes and emotions. A newly married couple most likely wants their own biological child, so adoption doesn't occur to them. But a childless couple who can't conceive may desperately want to adopt a child. For some, adoption is an opportunity to have a family without a spouse being required. On the other side of the situation, a birth mother who is unable or unwilling to care for her child may want to give up her child for adoption. The common denominator in all these situations is the child. The best place for a child to grow up is within a family. Connecting a child with a family so he or she will be nurtured and loved is a process filled with decisions, emotions, and hopes.

With God, the decision to adopt us wasn't hard at all. He wanted us in His forever family! Every person is a creation of God, but not every person is a child of God. Each of us is a physical person—the result of the union of a man and a woman. Even though we're physically alive, we are born spiritually dead in our transgressions (Ephesians 2:1). We are cut off from God.

The greatest news of all is that God the Father set up the adoption process by sending Jesus to die for our sins. Adopting us cost Christ His life. What a priceles opportunity for us to become God's child. When we put our faith in Him for salvation, the Spirit enters our lives. We're made spiritually alive and are no longer enslaved to sin. We're "born again."

And at that moment, God adopts us into His family. So now we can call Him "*Abba*," which means "Daddy." God the Father is our Daddy forever. When we're adopted, we receive all the rights and privileges of our new family. As sons and daughters of God, we can now live bearing the qualities of our Father.

Question for Today: Have you been adopted into God the Father's family? If yes, what are some of your privileges as an adopted child?

Prayer: Thank You, Father, that I can call You *Abba*. You've given me an eternal family, and I am amazed and so deeply grateful. Help me live like Your child.

Lord of Both the Living and the Dead
Let's Get Along

If we live, we live for the Lord; and if we die, we die for the Lord. So, whether we live or die, we belong to the Lord. For this very reason, Christ died and returned to life so that he might be the Lord of both the dead and the living (Romans 14:8-9).

FYI: There were many Christians living in Rome, coming from a variety of backgrounds. Some had been converted from paganism. These people refused to eat meat that had been sacrificed to idols. Other believers didn't have a problem with eating it. Not everyone observed the same holidays. With such diversity, they were having a hard time getting along.

People have different ways of behaving and doing things. Even among believers it can be hard to get along. Church history is loaded with disagreements, congregational splits, and personality clashes.

God doesn't say we all have to follow the same customs or personal habits. It's easy to get legalistic and say things like, "I can't believe they're doing that and still call themselves Christians." It doesn't matter if you like to sing hymns with an organ and someone else likes to sing praise songs with drums and guitars. If everyone loves Christ and are wholeheartedly following Him, behavior differences shouldn't be an issue. This glorious truth applies to all believers in Christ. Social habits and customs may be different, but we are all heirs to the Promise. The opportunity for fellowship in Christ is open to everyone.

We need to accept other believers despite our differences. Heaven is promised to *all believers in Christ*, regardless of customs, personal habits, ethnicity, and personalities (Romans 14:1-6). If we've accepted Christ as our Lord and Savior, we are not alone. "Whether we live or die, we belong to the Lord" (verse 8). Christ is the Lord of all living and dead believers. So let's all get along and enthusiastically serve Him together.

Question for Today: Are you having trouble liking another Christian because of personal or social issues?

Prayer: Christ, I'm so glad You are Lord of both the living and the dead. Help me live for You and encourage others to do the same.

God and Father of
Our Lord Jesus Christ
Our Ultimate Goal in Life

*May the God who gives endurance and encouragement give
you the same attitude of mind toward each other that Christ
Jesus had, so that with one mind and one voice you may glorify
the God and Father of our Lord Jesus Christ (Romans 15:6).*

FYI: After all the teachings on the complexity and simplicity of the
gospel, Paul wanted to make sure that the believers put their reasoned faith into practical actions. He wanted them to know that the
ultimate goal of the gospel is to glorify God the Father.

Building unity among Christians can be a daunting task. Getting along
with others is always a challenge, especially when we're very different from
each other. Unity with some Christian believers might seem impossible
at first glance. During these challenging times, we have a choice: We can
become upset with them or we can choose a different way.

Jesus Christ routinely told His disciples that living the Christian
life required hardship and sacrifice. He emphasized the purpose behind
becoming humble—that ultimately God the Father would be glorified.
Jesus spoke often of His close relationship with His heavenly Father. There
was nothing Jesus would do apart from Him. As part of the trinity, Jesus
was always in perfect unity with God the Father and the Holy Spirit.

Building unity among His followers is on Jesus' heart. And Paul prays
for God to give believers an attitude of endurance and encouragement.
We need endurance to be patient with each other. It doesn't come easy
sometimes—working together using our strengths to help others with
their weaknesses and vice versa. Encouragement is greatly needed because
it lifts our souls and motivates us to do more for God and His kingdom.

As you "bear with the failings of the weak" and choose to build up
the Christians around you, you're working to bring unity among believers
(Romans 15:1). The God and Father of our Lord Jesus Christ will be glorified.

Question for Today: Are you having trouble getting along with anyone? What makes it difficult to bear with the failings of someone you dislike?

Prayer: God and Father of my Lord, Jesus Christ, thank You for Your close relationship with Your Son, Jesus, and the Holy Spirit. Help me work with other Christians so we will be unified in glorifying You.

God of Hope
When Life Stinks

May the God of hope fill you with all joy and peace as you trust in him, so that you may overflow with hope by the power of the Holy Spirit (Romans 15:13).

FYI: This is the only time in the Bible "God of Hope" appears. Paul wants the Christians in Rome to stand on the solid foundation of God's provisions and know they are recipients of God's grace through faith in Christ.

Some days it's difficult to have hope. We even feel hopeless. On those despairing days we need to focus on God's unchanging truth: We can depend on Him because He is our God of hope. When Jesus went to be with the Father after His resurrection, He told believers He would be with them *always* (Matthew 28:20). The Holy Spirit would also remind believers that God was with them. No matter what happened, no matter what suffering or pain they endured, no matter the confusion that would ensue—believers could trust that God was at work in them and with them.

The Holy Spirit can't be thwarted by circumstances. Even in our most hopeless moments, we can have joy and peace in Him. We can trust the truth of God's Word. The God of hope gives us confidence in Him, and the Holy Spirit delivers this assurance with power. We may be crying, but even then we can cling to the eternal hope God gives.

Question for Today: What will you do the next time you feel hopeless? When you hit the wall of discouragement or you fall into the pit of depression, where will you seek a solution?

Prayer: God of hope, when I feel despair, fill me with Your hope, joy, and peace. You are the only one who has the answers to the deepest questions of life.

God of Peace
Living an Unpopular Message

The God of peace will soon crush Satan under your feet. The grace of our Lord Jesus be with you (Romans 16:20).

FYI: Believers in Jesus Christ in Rome were hated for following an invisible God. They were considered "atheists" because they didn't worship the idols around the city. For that, they were persecuted and murdered. Even in those perilous times, they remained faithful through the peace and hope God gave them.

There's a popular saying journalists like to repeat: "Don't kill the messenger!" Journalists report the news, but they don't create the conflicts that make the news. Still, many reporters feel the brunt of blame. Jesus delivered the news that grace, love, security, and salvation were available through Him. However, those who rejected Him would suffer eternal separation from God. As a result, Jesus was hated and vilified.

Living among people who don't believe, we also may experience similar rejection, misunderstandings, and mockery. When we do, God promised to empower us to live for Him, and someday He would crush Satan under our feet. When we choose to obey God, our actions may produce opposition. We can still rejoice because God gives us His peace.

Question for Today: Do you want to live like those without God, be accepted by them, and end up like them? Or do you want to live for Christ in His peace even if it means being persecuted?

Prayer: God of peace, thank You for promising that Satan will be defeated someday. Help me experience Your presence—including Your love, power, and grace—in my life today. Give me courage to share with people how thay can find Your peace and strength.

Deity
What Is God Like?

In Christ all the fullness of the Deity lives
in bodily form (Colossians 2:9).

FYI: This is the only time in the Bible that this name appears. The Greek word *pleroma* (translated "fullness") means "completeness, entirety, everything is included." The Colossian believers were being tempted to listen to false teachers with "hollow and deceptive philosophies," so they needed to know that Christ was fully God—not just 10 percent, or 50 percent, or even 99 percent. They needed to know that Jesus demonstrated God's character and ways.

Does God exist? Lots of people ask this question. In fact, many have given up trying to find the answer. They call themselves atheists. They claim there is no God, and that we are here on Earth for a time, die, and that's it. But is there nothing beyond what we see and feel on Earth? If there is a God, wouldn't it be great to know what He's like? He would need to communicate in such a way that each person could potentially understand His attributes and actions. And that's what He did! If we want to know what God is like, we need only to look at Christ. Jesus embodied the essence of God so that people could know His character, actions, purposes, and will.

When people make statements that go against what Christ said, they are speaking against God. When they do things contrary to what Christ did, they are disobeying God. The more we study about Christ, the more we'll understand God and follow Him instead of the ways of the world. When we are living for Christ, we are living for God.

Question for Today: Do you believe Christ is the visible expression of the invisible God?

Prayer: Oh matchless Deity, when I look at Jesus Christ, I see You. Through Him You have offered me a relationship with Yourself. Because You and Christ are one and I have given my life to Him, the fullness of the triune God (God the Father, God the Son, and God the Holy Spirit) lives in me. Praise You!

Spirit of Wisdom and Revelation
Thinking Outside Your Human Box

I keep asking that the God of our Lord Jesus Christ, the glorious Father, may give you the Spirit of wisdom and revelation, so that you may know him better (Ephesians 1:17).

FYI: This is the only time that the names "Spirit of Wisdom and Revelation" and "Glorious Father" are found in the Bible. In Isaiah 11:2, three other names are given that appear nowhere else—"Spirit of wisdom and of understanding, the Spirit of counsel and of might, the Spirit of the knowledge and fear of the LORD." The Holy Spirit embodies all these—and He lives in us!

When we move, get new jobs, or find a different church, meeting new friends is a major endeavor. Who wants to be friendless and lonely? But how do we really get to know a person? There are many ways, but the process includes spending time together, asking questions, listening, finding common interests, and doing activities together. All these help us make new friends. The same is true in getting to know God better.

Getting to know our glorious heavenly Father is a wonderful, lifelong pursuit. First, we have to meet God. This takes place when we put our faith in Christ's death and resurrection for us. The Spirit of wisdom and revelation enters our hearts and adopts us into God's forever family. Just like a baby is first born and then grows gradually into an adult, so we too, after we receive salvation, begin the process of learning more about God.

The only thing we can know about our glorious Father is what the Spirit of wisdom and revelation reveals. As we trust the Spirit to empower us to put into action what we're learning, we will grow in wisdom and godliness. Whatever we know now, we need to pray that the Spirit will teach us even more and pray for Christian friends to do the same.

Question for Today: What have you learned recently from the Spirit of wisdom and revelation?

Prayer: Spirit of wisdom and revelation, teach me to know my Father and the Lord Jesus Christ more intimately and to please them each day.

Chief Cornerstone
The Most Important Stone
in God's Building

[You are] fellow citizens with God's people and also
members of his household, built on the foundation of
the apostles and prophets, with Christ Jesus himself
as the chief cornerstone (Ephesians 2:19-20).

FYI: This significant concept was presented in Psalm 118:22 and, later, in Isaiah 28:16. More than 700 years later, Jesus enhanced its meaning (Matthew 21:42; Mark 12:10). Peter clearly proclaims that Jesus is the rejected cornerstone (Acts 4:11). Paul expands the teaching that God is constructing a spiritual building with Jesus as the chief cornerstone in today's verses.

The next time you walk by a stone or brick building, stop and look for the cornerstone. Today, cornerstones sometimes are marked with inscriptions or plaques naming the architect of the building and the date it was constructed. A cornerstone is a unique and critical part of a building. When it's laid on the foundation, it becomes the main measurement used to lay the rest of the stones or bricks. For that reason, it's considered the most important stone. The cornerstone determines the structure and the direction of the building—forever. Amazing that all that importance is in one block, isn't it? God called His Son, Jesus, "a chosen and precious cornerstone" (1 Peter 2:6).

Unpacking the cornerstone analogy gives us a greater picture of who Jesus Christ was in relation to the people He served. He may have seemed like an ordinary person on the outside. He lived among the poorest of the poor and among those who were rejected by society. But despite His simple outward appearance, Jesus was and continues to be a unique and critical part of the kingdom of God. Without Jesus, there would be no salvation or eternal life for humanity.

Just like a builder aligns all other blocks in relation to the cornerstone, God brings together believers from around the world and from all history to align us according to Christ. God is building a magnificent, heavenly temple in the Lord. Jesus is essential for the direction of what

God is building. All believers, including you and me, become "like living stones...built into a spiritual house" (1 Peter 2:5). In Christ, everything fits together perfectly. We are part of God's holy temple.

Question for Today: Is Jesus the chief Cornerstone of your life?

Prayer: Chief Cornerstone, if anything in my life is out of alignment, please show me so I can confess it to You and receive forgiveness. I want to be exactly who You want me to be.

God Our Savior
The Purpose of Peace

This is good, and pleases God our Savior (1 Timothy 2:3).

FYI: Timothy tried to pastor the church at Ephesus, but it was a difficult task for a man who was timid. Paul commanded him to be bold for the Lord and to use his talents and past experiences to build up the believers. There were some men who rejected their faith in Jesus and did awful things. Paul "handed [them] over to Satan to be taught not to blaspheme" (1 Timothy 1:20).

God's design for following and worshipping Him was never for just one person. His design always has reflected community. He chose the church body—with all its many unique and different parts—to be the major place for learning what it means to follow and worship Him.

There's a reason why community is stressed so much in Christian living. The meaning of "God our Savior" is "our only hope for salvation." Without embracing God, no one has hope for eternal life in heaven. Living in community with other believers, supporting each other, praying for God's provision in the midst of adversity—all of these actions are pleasing to God our Savior, "who wants all people to be saved and to come to a knowledge of the truth" (1 Timothy 2:4). They also help bring people to the realization of their need for Him.

God's design for believers is to encourage each other through everyday life. God's deepest desire is for all men and women to worship Him. Political and social peace allow the gospel to be spread to give hope to broken people in desperate need of God's healing and provision. God our Savior truly is the only way for people to come to the knowledge of truth.

Question for Today: Describe how Christ is the only way to God.

Prayer: God my Savior, thank You that You are my hope—the only One I need. I pray for my nation and those in authority. I want them to seek You and promote peace so many other people will come to the knowledge of the truth...of You.

Ruler
There Is Only One

*Take hold of the eternal life to which you were called...until
the appearing of our Lord Jesus Christ, which God will bring
about in his own time—God, the blessed and only Ruler, the
King of kings and Lord of lords (1 Timothy 6:12,14-15).*

FYI: Although the word "ruler" appears 176 times in the Bible, it's used
as a name of God only three times: 1 Timothy 6:15; Revelation 1:5; 3:14.
Even though the world is in turmoil, God ultimately rules. As a young
man, Timothy was facing all kinds of personal and professional challenges. He needed to be assured of the absolute governing power of
God. Timothy needed to know he was serving the "only Ruler."

Maranatha is an Aramaic word meaning "Lord come." In a troubled world
filled with turmoil, it's easy to long for God's redemption. You may catch
glimpses of suffering as you drive your car around your city. You may sense
it when you reach out to someone who is grieving or discouraged. You may
mourn with those who mourn about the losses and tragedies in their lives.
But you may struggle inside yourself as well.

These are the defining times of your life. They seem to call out to you,
urging you to reach up to God to get out of feelings of inadequacy and
weakness. You feel incapable of straightening the crooked paths and getting your life together. How can you help others if you can't help yourself?
Paul commands Timothy, "Fight the good fight of faith. Take hold of the
eternal life to which you were called" (1 Timothy 6:12). Life is a struggle—
especially against wrong and evil. But we're to fight for right until the Lord
Jesus Christ comes back. Look to Him who is immortal and lives in "unap-
proachable light" (verse 16). Our humanity prevents us from fully understanding Him and His ways, but we can trust that He rules! Behind the
chaos there is ultimate order.

God is the "only Ruler." There is no one above Him. He is the supreme
authority. He will make all things right. The next time you experience
struggles and great pressure, reach up and out. Reach up to God, and
reach out to others in need. Cry for the King of kings and Lord of lords
to return. *Maranatha!* Urge the only Ruler to make things right—to rule

with His mighty hand. What perfect peace this world will know when one day His children can say, "Our Lord and only Ruler has come!"

Question for Today: In your heart, do you cry *Maranatha!* to the one Ruler?

Prayer: Only Ruler, I trust You to reign in my heart. Help me trust You for victories in the good fights for justice, mercy, and peace. Show me how to do my part to help others in need. I want to reach up to You and out to others. *Maranatha!*

Master
Going from Wood to Gold

*Those who cleanse themselves from [wickedness]...will be
instruments for special purposes, made holy, useful to the
Master and prepared to do any good work (2 Timothy 2:21).*

FYI: The word translated "Master" appears 199 times in the Bible.
Seven times in the book of Luke, Jesus is referred to as Master. But
each time it is referring to His leadership. Master was an honored title
for a great person. Only 3 times does "Master" refer to God in heaven
(Ephesians 6:9; Colossians 4:1; and 2 Timothy 2:21).

Master artisans are experts in their fields. Artisans use the finest materials—gold, platinum, jewels, precious gems—to make precious works of art. Other craftspeople and manufacturers produce ordinary objects for a home—toilet bowl brushes, floor mats, rags, dustpans, and paper towels. Although these items are useful, their monetary value is far less than a precious ring. If someone gave you a choice to receive a diamond ring or a toilet bowl brush for free, which would you choose? The Bible sets the scene for this choice: "In a large house there are articles not only of gold and silver, but also of wood and clay; some are for special purposes and some for common use" (2 Timothy 2:20).

You are God's masterpiece made of priceless materials more precious than gold and silver. The Master wants to use you to change the lives of others, to draw the suffering into His arms, to bring His light into every situation for His glory and for your developing holiness. God, the Master, has great plans to use you to extend His handiwork to other people. He's prepared you "to do any good work" (2 Timothy 2:21). To be fully used by God, you must cleanse yourself from those things in your life that drag you down.

Question for Today: What needs to be purged from your life so you can become the Master's priceless instrument for good?

Prayer: Magnificent Master, my deepest desire is to be useful to You in whatever way You choose. Clean up the junk in my life that prevents You from using me fully. Make me clean and productive for Your glory.

Father of the Heavenly Lights
Gifts That Prove His Love for You

*Every good and perfect gift is from above, coming
down from the Father of the heavenly lights, who does
not change like shifting shadows (James 1:17).*

FYI: This is the only time "Father of the heavenly lights" occurs in the Bible, but the word "sun" appears 148 times, and "moon" appears 69 times. Psalm 136:3-9 says:

Give thanks to the Lord of lords...
>who made the great lights—His love endures forever.
>the sun to govern the day, His love endures forever.
>the moon and stars to govern the night;
>>His love endures forever.

When you look up in the sky on a cloudless day, you see the bright sun. The sun is so large that more than 330,000 Earths could fit inside it. It's so large that it accounts for about 99.86 percent of the mass in our solar system. The sun is absolutely essential for human life, and yet we take it for granted. We assume it will be there each day. What if one day the sun isn't there? What a crazy thought. All of life would cease.

Earth's only satellite in our sky is the moon. On some nights it looks very brilliant. Actually, it's dark, but it looks bright because it reflects the bright light of the sun. Besides lighting up the night sky, the moon affects the ocean tides. Aren't you glad the sun and the moon exist?

The bigger question, though, is where did the sun and moon (our two heavenly lights) come from? The Bible clearly states they came from the creative activity of God (Genesis 1:16; Psalm 136:7). The sun and moon are always in our sky even if clouds block our view. Our Creator made them and set up the laws of the universe, including our solar system. The sun and moon are good and perfect gifts from our Father of the heavenly lights. He doesn't make them shine today and shut them off tomorrow. Since He's given those humongous heavenly bodies to us for our existence, they show His kindness and steadfast love.

When the sun or moon is shining brightly, we can see our shadows. As we move, so does our shadow. The sun or moon is steady, but shadows move as the objects that the sun and/or the moon are shining on move. Our heavenly Father isn't like those shifting shadows. He is faithful even more than the rising of the sun and the setting of the moon.

God is light (1 John 1:5). Someday, in heaven, the sun and moon will no longer be needed because the glory of God will be the source of all light (Revelation 21:23; 22:5). What great light! What great love!

Question for Today: What good gifts has the Father of the heavenly lights given to you?

Prayer: The good and perfect gift You've given me, Father of the heavenly lights, is my life. But the greatest gift is eternal life through Your Son. You are so good!

Living Stone
Be Part of What God Is Building

As you come to him, the living Stone—rejected by humans
but chosen by God and precious to him—you...are
being built into a spiritual house (1 Peter 2:4-5).

FYI: The contrast inherent in this verse is amazing. Jesus said the builders of the temple rejected a stone to be the cornerstone of the temple (Matthew 21:42-44). He was that stone!

"Rejection." It's a painful word, a sad word, a hopeless word. You may experience rejection over and over again—and not just in a lifetime, but in a single day. That can get...well...more than discouraging. You don't get the job you wanted. The person you'd like to date doesn't like you back. Your child won't talk to you. Your family doesn't approve of your religion. Rejection hurts because it means someone is pushing you away. Throughout His ministry, Jesus was often rejected and despised—to the point of ultimately being murdered on the cross. But no—He is alive! Jesus is the living stone chosen by God to be the cornerstone of His kingdom. Discarded by people, but honored and glorified by God.

You too are His chosen. Regardless of how people treat you, when you come to the living Stone, God places you into His construction project. You become a vital part of a spiritual dwelling place for God. He molds you and builds you together with other believers. Now is the time to get serious with God and crave spiritual growth so you're sturdy enough for His building. Reject anything that makes you unfit for His project. Let Him pick you up like a brick and place you where you belong. If you trust in Christ, you'll "never be put to shame" (1 Peter 2:6).

Question for Today: Are you craving to grow in Christ?

Prayer: O precious living Stone, thank You for not rejecting me. I want to be a part of Your spiritual dwelling place. Please mold me and place me wherever You want.

Cornerstone
The Solution for Shame

*In Scripture it says: "See, I lay a stone in Zion, a chosen
and precious cornerstone, and the one who trusts in
him will never be put to shame" (1 Peter 2:6).*

FYI: Jesus Christ fulfills the description of the mysterious cornerstone in Isaiah 28:16; Matthew 21:42; Mark 12:10; Luke 20:17; Acts 4:11; Ephesians 2:20.

Watching people build a house piques our interest. As they clear the lot we wonder what kind of a house it will be. As the foundation is laid we can see the basic footprint and get a better idea of what to expect. With each section that's built, it becomes more evident what the house will look like. The mystery slowly disappears as the structure emerges.

Likewise, God is building a structure of which we are all a part, and Jesus is the cornerstone. Before Peter wrote his letter, the sovereign Lord said He was building a structure in Zion (Jerusalem) that had a foundation based on a precious cornerstone (Isaiah 28:16). For more than 700 years, the mystery of what God was building remained just that. Then after Jesus was raised from the dead, He was revealed as the foundational cornerstone!

The cornerstone is fundamental to a structure because all stones are laid in reference to it. The whole structure God is building relies on Jesus. If we trust Him for salvation and for the power to live a God-honoring life, we'll never be ashamed. Yes, we may experience shame for our sin and selfishness, but the blood of Jesus cleanses us. We can lift our heads and our hearts with thankfulness to Him. Give Christ your guilt and shame. He'll forgive you and make you a vital part of all that God is building.

Question for Today: Do you feel shame about anything in your life? Confess it and receive God's forgiveness. Move forward with confidence that Christ is guiding you to fulfill His purposes for you.

Prayer: Jesus, You are the precious Cornerstone of all that God is building. How thankful I am that You're totally trustworthy. I confidently follow You.

Overseer
The Best Manager Ever

*"You were like sheep going astray," but now you have returned
to the Shepherd and Overseer of your souls (1 Peter 2:25).*

FYI: Peter used "Overseer" as a name for God, which hadn't been used that way before, although the word was common for human leaders. In Exodus 5, "overseer" is used five times referring to leaders of Egypt and the Israelites. Paul tells the church leaders that they are guardians and shepherds of the flock of believers (Acts 20:28). He also warns that overseers must be blameless and trustworthy (1 Timothy 3:1-2).

The Bible calls us sheep for good reason. Sheep do stupid things like wander away from the shepherd in their search for food—only to become a meal for a wolf. Because of our independent attitude, we all go astray too (Isaiah 53:6). Peter describes Jesus as our "Shepherd and Overseer." Overseer means "to watch over." In the church it's used for one who watches over fellow believers. He is usually considered wise and experienced so he can help people make good choices and be in harmony with other Christ followers.

In today's verse, Peter was writing to the Christians scattered throughout the Roman Empire urging them to endure suffering and injustice like Christ did. We, like them, are to have His right attitude, to speak kindly, and to commit ourselves to the One who judges righteously (1 Peter 2:19-24).

The tendency of all humans is to get angry and vengeful when we're personally mistreated. We break away from God's leadership and example. The good news is that even when we think we're justified in our wrong attitudes, the Shepherd and Overseer hasn't let us out of His sight.

When we go our own way, we alienate our magnificent God. But when we give our wayward heart back to Him, our Shepherd and Overseer will produce in us the endurance and patience to handle whatever we're experiencing—if we entrust our circumstances to the Lord's will.

Question for Today: What has the Shepherd and Overseer guided you to do?

Prayer: Shepherd and Overseer, I'm sorry for wandering from You so often. I come back to You for forgiveness because I deeply desire Your leadership and guidance.

Spirit of Glory
Blessed Through Insults?

If you are insulted because of the name of Christ, you are blessed,
for the Spirit of glory and of God rests on you (1 Peter 4:14).

FYI: "Spirit of glory" appears only in this passage. Tradition states that after a large part of Rome was destroyed by fire in AD 64, the Emperor Nero blamed the Christians to deflect accusations directed toward him. As a result, Christians were hated, vilified, and tortured. Their deaths were treated as sport; often they were torn to pieces by wild animals for sport or hung on crosses and set on fire to serve as torches.

Have you served for any amount of time in an impoverished place—perhaps in an inner city or in another country? If so, you may have noticed the attitudes of some of the people. Often folks who live in poverty are able to thank God despite their pain, suffering, and hardship. Maybe you wondered how they could do that. Maybe you compared their attitudes with the ones of people you know who were living lives of abundance. What was your conclusion? And what is your attitude regarding hardships?

At some point in our lives, we all face extreme hardships. Though the hardships may be different, the feelings that come with them are universal. We may feel rejected, insulted, terrorized, abandoned, disrespected, or antagonized. There are many common feelings that come with life's difficulties.

Peter writes something very interesting about difficult times. He says we shouldn't be surprised when facing trials "as though something strange were happening to [us]" (1 Peter 4:12). He may have been commenting on the reality of the predicament of all Christians. Living in a fallen, imperfect world of pain and separation from God means we will face ridicule and insults at some point in our lives. But Peter also points out that no matter what the circumstance, we can guarantee our eternal bliss by rejoicing "that [we] participate in the sufferings of Christ" (verse 13). What sets us apart is that we belong to God. The "Spirit of glory" lives inside us and rests on us.

That means no matter what happens to us, those things can't touch what God has given us. This was the case for Jesus, whose body was mistreated and marred. No one could touch His Spirit. This revelation alone can help us face the hardships of life. We can live through them with joy deep inside as we anticipate Christ's return. Don't be ashamed to suffer for Christ! Continue to commit yourself to your "faithful Creator and continue to do good" (1 Peter 4:19).

Question for Today: Why are you blessed when you're insulted for believing in Christ?

Prayer: Spirit of glory, thank You for living inside me. Give me the confidence and the courage to rejoice despite my circumstances. Help me have a joyful and pleasant attitude when I'm unappriciated or insulted. I look forward to Your return!

Chief Shepherd
Leading by Love

When the Chief Shepherd appears, you will receive the
crown of glory that will never fade away (1 Peter 5:4).

FYI: Peter was aware that persecution and coercion can force people to deny Christ. He reminded them of the hope of Christ, their Chief Shepherd Leader. He will give the faithful an infinitely greater reward than anything on earth, so they should stay true to Him.

When we accept Jesus Christ into our hearts, we begin an amazing, life-changing relationship. God promises that He will never abandon us, that we will have everything we need, and that there's nothing we can do to make Him stop loving us. Although we may experience the hurts of a fallen world, our lives will, one day, be free of pain in heaven.

With that new relationship comes a responsibility to reach out in love to those who don't know Jesus. This isn't a burden forced on us by a controlling God. No! We experience something miraculous and transformative when we become Christians. Then we become eager to share Jesus' love with others. We long for people to know that this broken world is not all there is to life. We speak love out of our devotion to Christ.

Some Christians forget what it's like to love God in this way. They choose to follow their own ways and personal agendas. Peter encourages believers with an important truth: Christians who suffer yet who seek a God-honoring life don't need to be afraid. The Chief Shepherd, our Leader, will give Christians an "unfading crown of glory" when we submit our lives to Him and lead others in ways that reflect His heart.

Question for Today: Are you a Christ follower who reflects Him through your words and actions? How can you become a stronger leader for Christ?

Prayer: Chief Shepherd, teach me to be a leader like You. Help me be the kind of leader who pours Your truth into other people because I'm overflowing with You.

God of All Grace
Strength Through Suffering

The God of all grace, who called you to his eternal glory in Christ, after you have suffered a little while, will himself restore you and make you strong, firm and steadfast (1 Peter 5:10).

FYI: In the verses directly before today's verse, Peter exhorts believers to be on guard against the devil, who prowls around "like a roaring lion" looking for someone, anyone, to devour. Living in this world as Christians doesn't mean we'll be protected from the pains, the temptations, and the battles that come against our souls. Satan tries to destroy our faith and relationship with God. But God is greater!

Have you ever felt like God wasn't present? Like He didn't hear your prayers? Or, perhaps more honestly, that He couldn't care less about your concerns? In a world full of adversity, it's easy to connect circumstances with God. We live in a world in which evil really exists. Pain is a given, and poor moral choices can lead to painful consequences. In a physical body that is fallible and finite, it's easy to assume that God is distant. During times of deep suffering, we must fight to believe that He hasn't forgotten us or abandoned us. It's not possible for God to forget us. It goes against His very nature. He knows all. He sees all. He is all-powerful. He is the definition of love. He doesn't change no matter what our circumstances.

The "God of all grace" offers us hope we can believe in. He promises He will not leave us alone in this world. He's prepared a home for us with Him in heaven. He promises to take all of our pain, suffering, and adversity and redeem them. The God of all grace, whose name literally means "grace before all and beyond all," will use our trials to make us stronger, more confident, and, most especially, complete in Him. All that we suffer now, God will use to make us more like Him.

Question for Today: In what ways are your present sufferings making you more like God?

Prayer: God of all grace, thank You for making something beautiful out of all my brokenness. I'm thankful that You have a plan to make me more complete through all I endure in this life.

Majestic Glory
No Doubt

[Jesus Christ] received honor and glory from God the Father when the voice came to him from the Majestic Glory, saying, "This is my Son, whom I love; with him I am well pleased" (2 Peter 1:17).

FYI: Peter, James, and John went with Jesus up on a high mountain. When they saw Him transformed into His heavenly body, it shook them up. Then they heard the voice of God. They never forgot that— and they want all believers to know that Jesus is God.

Today it's difficult for many people to believe in the resurrection of Jesus Christ; sometimes, this is because those who doubt Jesus Christ's redemptive story were not eyewitnesses to His ministry and His resurrection. They're like those who say, "I'll believe it when I see it." But, of course, they can't go back in time and see those events in person. They have to trust the evidence others have presented.

Wanting evidence isn't wrong. Even Peter writes that the disciples "did not follow cleverly devised stories" when they told of the miraculous life of the Lord Jesus Christ (2 Peter 1:16). They were eyewitnesses to Christ's majesty. Right in front of them, they saw Him transfigured on the mountain, alongside Moses and Elijah (Matthew 17:2). Peter, James, and John were overwhelmed by what they saw and heard. When God, the Majestic Glory, whose name means "magnificent radiance," let the disciples know who Jesus really was—His Son—the Majestic Glory bestowed honor and glory on Jesus. God made it absolutely clear that He was pleased with Jesus, and that the disciples needed to listen to Him. Period. No frivolous pandering. No superficial promises. Just obey Jesus.

We can trust in God because of the witnesses who saw Jesus and spent time with Him. The many witnesses to Jesus' life, ministry, miracles, and resurrection bear truth through the Scriptures and give knowledge and confidence to doubting souls.

Question for Today: What are some of the doubts you have about God today?

Prayer: ...jestic Glory, shine Your radiance into my life. Open my eyes ...th of who You are. Let the dawn rise in my heart so that I might ...and believe even more.

Majesty in Heaven
Opulence out of This World

The Son is the radiance of God's glory and the exact representation of his being, sustaining all things by his powerful word. After he had provided purification for sins, he sat down at the right hand of the Majesty in heaven (Hebrews 1:3).

FYI: Majesty in reference to a name of God is used twice, both times in the book of Hebrews (Hebrews 1:3 and 8:1).

When you hear the word "opulence," what comes to mind? Maybe someone extremely rich who shows off his or her possessions? Maybe lots of gold and precious jewelry? Or a fabulous, glitzy, Hollywood show? Or a government ceremony for a visiting head of state? No matter how magnificent, those events can't rival the out-of-this-world beauty of the heavenly splendor of Majesty.

"Majesty in heaven" is the sovereign God who reigns supreme over the entire universe. The word "sovereignty" means "supreme." It carries the connotation of being extreme. God's sovereignty means that He is extremely supreme above all others in power, authority, and beauty.

God rules from His magnificent throne. This is the supreme God who laid the foundations of the world and made the heavens with His hands. This is the powerful God whose thoughts are higher than our thoughts, but who is still kind enough to care about what we think. This is the unchanging God whose throne will last forever and ever. He rules our universe with a scepter of righteousness.

The Majesty in heaven honored Jesus by seating Him right next to His throne. No one else can compete for that place. God the Father is far above all earthly beings. No earthly dignitary, Hollywood star, or billionaire can come close to His divine opulence. We will all die physically, but He lives eternally. He has not abandoned His throne, nor will He ever leave it. He is the Majesty in heaven, and no one can usurp God's sovereighty over all. Praise Him with all your heart and thank Him that someday you will reign with Him.

Question for Today: What does "Majesty in heaven" mean to you?

Prayer: Majesty in heaven, this world's opulence can't even minutely compare with all that is Yours. I praise You that Your beauty, magnificence, and glory will never fade.

High Priest
Bringing Us Together

*Since we have a great high priest who has ascended
into heaven, Jesus the Son of God, let us hold
firmly to the faith we profess (Hebrews 4:14).*

FYI: The three required offices of the Messiah were Prophet, Priest, and King. No Jew could hold all three positions. Priests could only come from the lineage of Levi, and kings could only come from the tribe of Judah. However, *Jesus* held all three. He was the Prophet; He was from the tribe of Judah; He was from the priestly line of Melchizedek (Hebrews 5:10).

Think of a serious dispute you've had with someone. It seemed irresolvable. Maybe you thought you and this other person really didn't understand each other—and that you could never work out your differences. Maybe you even considered calling in someone to hear both sides and mediate a solution.

That's really the way it was between God and humanity. We needed a mediator to build a bridge across the impassable chasm between God and us. Because of our sinful nature, we were spiritually dead to God (Ephesians 2:1-2).

In Bible times, among the Jewish people, the high priest was the chief priest of the temple. He was entrusted with the duty of entering the most sacred place of the temple—the Most Holy Place (Exodus 26:33, 1 Kings 6:16)—once a year. There he would sprinkle the blood of a goat as a sin offering for all the Jewish people, so they would be forgiven and receive right standing before their holy God (Leviticus 16; 23:26-32; Numbers 29:7-11).

The work of the high priest foreshadowed the work of Jesus on our behalf. The Son of God made the ultimate sacrifice. On the cross, He shed His blood for all of humanity. Because of our sin, we all should die on crosses. Then we'd be physically *and* spiritually dead—eternally separated from God. Because Jesus was fully God and fully man, He is our High Priest, forgiving our sins and clearing the way for us to relate directly with God. Jesus has gone through the heavens to reach us and bring us to God.

Our Lord is able to sympathize with our weaknesses because He also felt them—although He didn't sin. The Son of God is our High Priest who makes it possible for us to have personal relationships with God forever.

Question for Today: Are you spiritually alive to God? Is He your High Priest?

Prayer: Son of God, my perfect High Priest, thank You for opening the way for me to have a relationship with God the Father. Thank You for Your death on the cross. I will praise You forever!

Spirit of Grace
Punishment Fits the Crime

How much more severely do you think someone deserves to be punished who has trampled the Son of God underfoot, who has treated as an unholy thing the blood of the covenant that sanctified them, and who has insulted the Spirit of grace? (Hebrews 10:29).

FYI: This passage is related to the unpardonable sin mentioned in Matthew 12:32; Mark 3:29; Luke 12:10. The "Spirit of grace" is also found in Zechariah 12:10, but the translators have used the article "a" instead of "the."

As much as we would like people to obey the laws and be good citizens, there are some people who just don't fit in. They carry a chip on their shoulder, exhibit angry dispositions, and radiate resentment. This is why we lock our doors at night. There are individuals who do evil things.

But what about in the spiritual realm? Yes, evil lurks there also. Corrupt, evil people who not only utterly despise Christ, but who maliciously slander God's gospel of love will have to account for their actions. God says they will be punished: "It is mine to avenge; I will repay" (Hebrews 10:30). "It is a dreadful thing to fall into the hands of the living God" (verse 31). If you know people like this, pray they will repent before it's too late.

Thankfully, the Son of God loved us so much that He gave His life so that we can have God's life in us. This is God's grace—that He freely gives us forgiveness and eternal life when we put our faith in Him. Thus, the Spirit of grace is the divine Giver through whom God's love is poured into the lives of sinners who repent of their sins.

Question for Today: How do you think God feels about people who trample the Son of God and insult the Spirit of grace?

Prayer: How kind and immensely gracious You are, Spirit of grace. You offer forgiveness to the vilest of sinners who humbly repent. I'm so grateful You've forgiven me.

Father of Spirits
Who Likes to Be Disciplined?

We have all had human fathers who disciplined us and we respected them for it. How much more should we submit to the Father of spirits and live! (Hebrews 12:9).

FYI: This is the only time this name is given. God disciplines us perfectly every time (Hebrews 12:4-12). His Word is "useful for teaching, rebuking, correcting and training in righteousness" (2 Timothy 3:16).

Think back to when you were growing up. You chose to do something you knew was wrong. You were told not to do it, but you did it anyway. How did your parents react toward you? Were they angry? Did they threaten you? Or maybe they spanked you, sent you to your room, made you go without dinner, or gave you the silent treatment.

Think about your thoughts and feelings as a result. Were you truly sorry for your actions or did you just pretend to be sorry? Did you rebel again later just to "show" them? What were your attitudes toward yourself? When you look back, are you glad you were corrected or do you still hold a grudge?

Now, consider how you react when God the Father disciplines you. Do you feel and react in a similar manner? When a child puts an object into his mouth that he found on the ground, a loving parent takes it away immediately because the child might choke or digest something bad. The child may scream and cry, indicating the belief that the parent doesn't love him, but the exact opposite is true. Parents discipline out of love and a desire for their child's welfare. God likewise disciplines us for our good—not because He hates us, but because He loves us and wants us to live the best life possible. Unlike our parents who were imperfect and failed many times, God is perfect. He corrects us just right every time. Why is He called the "Father of spirits"? Because when we sin and are disciplined, it's not pleasant so we may feel ashamed or become depressed. When we suffer the consequences of our wrong behavior, we may get angry at God. But, instead, we should put our faith in the perfect, loving Father who will comfort our spirit and give us true joy. He is the only guide who can show us how to make good changes so we can live in ways that please Him. We can't ask for anything better than that.

Question for Today: Is the Father of spirits disciplining you about something?

Prayer: Father of spirits, I don't like to be disciplined, but I know I need it because I often turn from You and my faith grows cold. Thank You for loving me so much that You look out for my welfare. I want to always walk close to You.

Great Shepherd of the Sheep
The Boss of Your Boss

*May the God of peace, who through the blood of the
eternal covenant brought back from the dead our Lord
Jesus, that great Shepherd of the sheep (Hebrews 13:20).*

FYI: This is the only time that Jesus is called the "great Shepherd of the sheep." The next verse says that Jesus will "equip you with everything good for doing his will." You have nothing to fear when you're an obedient sheep.

Jesus' life was one of compassion. He didn't deny people His love, healing power, or kindness. He loved those who were rejected, sinful, and sick. With deep caring, He reached out to people. His ultimate act of love was enduring an excruciating death on the cross so we can have a personal, loving relationship with our heavenly Father.

What do shepherds lead? Sheep. What are sheep like? They are helpless, defenseless, wanderers, dumb, and smelly. That describes us too. We need a strong, kind, and competent leader. That describes Jesus. We can trust Him because He hung on a tree and then rose from the dead for us. God says that He is the great Shepherd meaning that He is the greatest of all shepheards. There are lots of human "shepherds" who try to lead us. Some are bad and lead the sheep astray. Some are good and try to lead the sheep to follow God. But they all are human and prone to error. Jesus is the great Shepherd who leads us perfectly all the time. He is therefore worthy of our love, allegiance, and obedience. We can't go wrong following Him. He will lead us safely through times of joy and difficulty.

Question for Today: In what ways do you need the guidance of the great Shepherd right now?

Prayer: Great Shepherd of the sheep, I need Your compassionate nudging, guiding, and leading today. Show me the way as I go through my day and interact with others.

Word of Life
Living Proof of the Best Life

That which was from the beginning, which we have
heard, which we have seen with our eyes, which we
have looked at and our hands have touched—this we
proclaim concerning the Word of life (1 John 1:1).

FYI: The Bible describes three beginnings: 1) the beginning of creation (Genesis 1:1), 2) the beginning of everything (John 1:1-3), and 3) the beginning of Jesus' life on earth (1 John 1:1). Before each of these, Jesus already existed.

To be "living proof" of the best life means that someone is an example of a truth. It could refer to an experience: "The way they love each other is living proof that marriage can make you happy." "Living proof" might also show evidence that something difficult was achieved: "If you think that a thirty-year-old car can't go over 130 miles per hour, that last race is living proof it can be done." Another use of the phrase is showing the validity of a saying: "She's living proof that life begins at forty."

When you consider the idea of living life to the fullest, who would you guess has done it the best? Yes, there have been many people who have lived magnificent and productive lives. But without a doubt, the supreme example of someone living the best quality of life is Jesus Christ. He's living proof of what it means to "walk with God."

The apostle John wrote three short letters near the end of his life (1 John, 2 John, 3 John). When they were written, circa AD 85-90, John had witnessed firsthand many powerful leaders who acted questionably, including Roman governor Pilate, Jewish High Priest Caiaphas, and Roman General Titus, who destroyed Jerusalem and the Jewish temple in AD 70.

One of the first four disciples to follow Jesus, John watched the way Jesus conducted His life from the very beginning of His ministry (Mark 1:19-20). He heard the sermons and conversations Jesus Christ shared. John witnessed Jesus performing many miracles. When Jesus related to the people who followed Him and to the people who hated Him, John watched. He touched the bread that was miraculously multiplied to feed 5,000 men (Mark 6:30-44), and he was the one who leaned against Jesus' breast during the Passover supper before His crucifixion (John 13:21-25). When Jesus was on the cross, John was so close that Christ could tell him to take care of His mother (John 19:26-27).

With greater personal knowledge and experience of Jesus during His ministry than anyone else, John was convinced Jesus was the Word of Life, meaning He was the embodiment and messenger of life itself. John believed Jesus created all life and showed the way for us to live (John 1:1-3). Because He was holy and perfect in every way, Jesus is the living proof that the best life is found in God alone.

Question for Today: How would you describe Jesus as the "Word of life"?

Prayer: Dear Jesus, You demonstrated convincingly that you are the Word of life. Grant me the courage and the wisdom to proclaim the truth about You to anyone who will listen.

The First and the Last
Overwhelmed by Divinity

When I saw him, I fell at his feet as though dead. Then he placed his right hand on me and said: "Do not be afraid. I am the First and the Last" (Revelation 1:17).

FYI: "The First and the Last" is mentioned only two other times, in Revelation 2:8; 22:13.

When you suddenly come face-to-face with a very important person you never expected to see, what is your reaction? Do you suddenly shy away or do you excitedly burst out an exclamation of amazement? How would you react if you met God that way? Look how others reacted. Moses hid his face (Exodus 3:6), Joshua fell facedown (Joshua 5:14), and Isaiah exclaimed, "Woe to me!…I am ruined!" (Isaiah 6:5). Ezekiel fell facedown too (Ezekiel 1:28), and Daniel was terrified and fell prostrate (Daniel 8:17; 10:9-11). And what about John?

> When I turned I saw seven golden lampstands, and among the lampstands was someone like a son of man, dressed in a robe reaching down to his feet and with a golden sash around his chest. The hair on his head was white like wool, as white as snow, and his eyes were like blazing fire. His feet were like bronze glowing in a furnace, and his voice was like the sound of rushing waters. In his right hand he held seven stars, and coming out of his mouth was a sharp, double-edged sword. His face was like the sun shining in all its brilliance (Revelation 1:12-16).

John was so overwhelmed and frightened that he fainted (Revelation 1:17). Wouldn't you? John had been the closest to Jesus on Earth, but now the Lord was totally different. He was the divine Christ, the First and the Last stunningly glorified. He existed before the furthest point back in the past and will exist beyond the furthest point in the future. *Jesus is God.* There was no one before Him, and there will be no one after Him. Love and obey Him because someday you'll meet Him face-to-face.

Question for Today: What would you do if you suddenly met this spectacular Person described by John?

Prayer: The First and the Last, I fall at Your feet overwhelmed by Your glory.

Living One
The Keys to Eternal Death

*I am the Living One; I was dead, and now look, I
am alive for ever and ever! And I hold the keys
of death and Hades (Revelation 1:18).*

FYI: When we're in heaven, Jesus will transform our bodies so we'll be like Him (Philippians 3:20-21; 1 John 3:1-3). The word "Hades" means the place of death and is found only in the New Testament.

The Bible contains God's revelation about heaven. Christ came from heaven, and He told us about it and how to get there. John, the writer of the book of Revelation, described how he received a vision of heaven. God "made it known by sending his angel to his servant John" (Revelation 1:1). God opened the window to the future and let John look in. And the disciple wrote about what he saw.

John had seen Jesus on Earth. He had witnessed the beatings He received from the Jewish leaders and Roman soldiers. He was right there at the cross observing Jesus' final moments. After His resurrection John was overjoyed (John 20:19-20). However, when he saw Jesus, the eternal Living One, in heaven, he was so completely awestruck that he fell at His Lord's feet (Revelation 1:17). Jesus isn't only the possessor of life forever, but He also holds authority over death. If you've given your life to Him, you don't have to fear death. God will change your perishable body into an imperishable one and defeat death (1 Corinthians 15:50-58). He's given you a new life that will never end. He can enliven every aspect of your life and free you from anything that tries to pull you down.

Question for Today: Do you fear death? Why or why not?

Prayer: Living One, how I praise You for providing new life to me while I'm on Earth and eternal life in heaven.

Jesus' New Name
A Very Surprising Reward

The one who is victorious I will make a pillar in the temple of my God. Never again will they leave it. I will write on them the name of my God and the name of the city of my God, the new Jerusalem, which is coming down out of heaven from my God; and I will also write on them my new name (Revelation 3:12).

FYI: Christ has promised many surprises when He comes back. You can read about some of the coming rewards He promises in Psalm 62:12; Matthew 16:27; 1 Corinthians 3:10-15; 9:25.

Jesus has a big surprise for His faithful followers. In His message to the angel of the church in Philadelphia, Jesus commends those who have obeyed His commands and endured persecution patiently (Revelation 3:8-10). Even though the believers were weak while facing hardship, they didn't deny His name or cave in to their persecutors. The Lord gives grace to those going through trying times and strengthens them in the midst of trials.

God urges His followers to hold on to what they have in Him and confidently trust His promises. In the time set by God, the Lord will come back to Earth to conquer His enemies and demonstrate that He is the supreme Ruler. Then He'll unveil the secret treasures He's reserved for all who have truly followed Him. These rewards and honors are unimaginable to our finite minds. Jesus has also promised to write on them God's name and the name of the New Jerusalem (Revelation 3:12). Amazing! But the real shock comes when Jesus reveals His new name and writes it on you and me. What an incredible secret—and we'll possess His new name for all eternity. *Wow!*

Question for Today: Are you keeping God's command to endure patiently?

Prayer: Lord Jesus, keep me close to You. Give me strength and patience to endure hardship because I know You'll be returning soon in victory.

Amen
The "Yes" of God Is Speaking

*To the angel of the church in Laodicea write: "These are
the words of the Amen, the faithful and true witness,
the ruler of God's creation" (Revelation 3:14).*

FYI: The word "amen" appears 57 times from the book of Numbers to
the book of Revelation. It's often used at the end of statements about
the Lord. Psalm 89:52 says, "Praise be to the LORD forever! Amen and
Amen." Today's passage is the only place in Scripture that "Amen" is
used as a proper name. Paul exclaimed, "No matter how many promises God has made, they are 'Yes' in Christ. And so through him the
'Amen' is spoken by us to the glory of God" (2 Corinthians 1:20).

When you hear someone make a statement that you enthusiastically agree
with, what do you say? There are many different expressions people use to
give their hearty approval. It depends on what your friends say, your ethnicity, family habits, age, and religious faith. I'm sure you recognize these:
"Awesome!" "You bet!" "Right on!" "Cool!" "You got it!" "Okay!" "So be
it!" "Yes!"

These expressions are used to show confirmation and solidarity. The
Bible has an expression that shows total agreement too: the word "amen."
People throughout the Bible said "Amen" to express their heartfelt accep-
tance and endorsement of a statement or command. The Hebrews used
"amen" to agree with Moses about giving God's law (Deuteronomy
27:15-26). Benaiah responded with an "amen" to King David's promise concerning the reign of his son Solomon (1 Kings 1:36). With an
"amen," Jeremiah endorsed what the Lord promised Israel (Jeremiah 11:5).
Throughout the Bible people interjected "Amen!" when God's truth was
proclaimed.

The people in the church in Laodicea were neither hot nor cold toward
the Lord. They were lukewarm—noncommittal, plain vanilla. They were
rich but didn't care about the poor. They were comfortable in their situation, and blind to their pride and arrogance. Christ wanted to shake them
out of their lethargy. "These are the words of the Amen" means that Jesus
is the affirmation of all God's truth. He is faithful. He rules God's creation.

So wake up! He rebukes offenders, but lives in those who receive Him. The "Amen" is speaking!

Question for Today: Are you listening to the Amen?

Prayer: Oh Amen, my heart so easily grows cold when I slip into my spiritual comfort zone. Wake me up so I'll see the needs of the people around me.

Lion of the Tribe of Judah
First Comes the Lamb and
Then Comes the Lion

One of the elders said to me [John], "Do not weep! See, the Lion of the tribe of Judah, the Root of David, has triumphed. He is able to open the scroll and its seven seals" (Revelation 5:5).

FYI: The word "lion" appears 135 times in the Bible.

About 100 years ago there were more than 200,000 lions roaming the savannahs and grasslands. Lions used to be the most widespread, large, land mammal after humans. But they have disappeared from 80 percent of their historic range due to habitat loss and conflicts with humans. Today there are fewer than 30,000 lions living in the wild. Lions used to roam the forests and deserts throughout the Middle East, although there are none there now except in zoos.

Lions were greatly feared throughout the Old Testament, and they were often used as a symbol of destruction. Warning of the coming devastation to rebellious northern Israel, Amos predicted, "This is what the LORD says: 'As a shepherd rescues from the lion's mouth only two leg bones or a piece of an ear, so will the Israelites living in Samaria be rescued, with only the head of a bed and a piece of fabric from a couch'" (Amos 3:12). Psalm 22 foreshadows the coming Messiah and what will happen to Him. Although the cross had most likely not been used for executions yet, this psalm depicts accurately what was going to happen to Jesus. As He was dying, our Messiah quoted from this psalm: "My God, my God, why have you forsaken me?" Later in the psalm is this lament: "Roaring lions that tear their prey open their mouths wide against me" (Psalm 22:13). Jesus gave His life to the ravenous beasts of Rome.

But the book of Revelation reveals a vastly different side. The Messiah is the ravenous Lion of the tribe of Judah. He devours His enemies and celebrates victory over the ungodly. Lion heads were often carved into a king's throne to show royalty and power. In heaven, the Lion lives and is majestically ruling the world. The writer of the book of Revelation, John, weeps because no one can open the scroll of God's wrath. He was told the

Lion of the tribe of Judah can. When John looked, he saw the Lamb (Revelation 5:5-7). Jesus is both Lion and Lamb. A lion was emblazoned on the banner of Judah, the tribe from which all Jewish kings came. Jesus is all-powerful, majestic, and sovereign.

Question for Today: Why do you think the Lion of the tribe of Judah was able to break the seals and open the scroll?

Prayer: Jesus, You are the Lion of the tribe of Judah—majestic, all-powerful, and triumphant over all Your enemies. I worship You and sing Your praises with my whole being.

Faithful and True
It's Not Science Fiction

I saw heaven standing open and there before me was a
white horse, whose rider is called Faithful and True. With
justice he judges and makes war (Revelation 19:11).

FYI: Jesus Christ is identified as "Faithful and True" first in Revelation 3:14. The words "faithful," "faithfulness," and "faithfully" appear 465 times in Bible. God is faithful, and He wants us to be faithful to Him.

Every 92 minutes, Old Faithful, a geyser in Yellowstone National Park, erupts and shoots boiling water more than 145 feet in the air. Old Faithful is one of the most predictable geographical features on Earth. However, since it was discovered in 1870 the intervals between eruptions have slowly increased from 66 minutes to today's average of 92.

Far more accurate is an atomic clock that has an "uncertainty" of one second in 30 million years. Even though that is incredibly precise, there is still an element of inexactness.

There is something infinitely more accurate than Old Faithful and an atomic clock. Actually, it is not a something—it's a Someone. And He will come out of heaven to wage war against the enemies of God. His character is perfectly faithful and true. After the disobedience of Adam and Eve, the world has been tainted with imperfection. But God is absolutely perfect and He is Faithful. His Word is accurate in every way. Coupled with faithfulness is truth. God is the exact definition of truth without any distortion.

"The beast and the kings of the earth and their armies gathered together to wage war against the rider on the horse and his army" (Revelation 19:19). The beast is the Antichrist, who rules the world through the great tribulation. However, when Faithful and True comes, He will defeat him and his false prophet, who swayed the world against God. They will be thrown into the fiery lake, and their armies will be killed (verses 20-21). The forces of evil will be defeated. Faithful and True absolutely guarantees it.

Question for Today: Have you found God to be faithful and true?

Prayer: Jesus, You are Faithful and True and do exactly what You promise. You will defeat the Antichrist and his evil followers. May it happen soon.

Jesus' Private Name
A Surprise Ending

His eyes are like blazing fire, and on his head are
many crowns. He has a name written on him that
no one knows but he himself (Revelation 19:12).

FYI: Revelation 19 starts with all of heaven praising and worshipping God while preparing for the wedding supper of the Lamb. Then suddenly heaven opens up, and Jesus rides out triumphantly to wage war against His enemies, especially the Antichrist. Jesus has a name no one knows except Him. Even if we never know the full meaning of His secret name, we know this is Jesus. His victory over Satan will be displayed for all to see.

Have you ever gone to a surprise birthday party? You may remember the excitement you had as you hid in the dark waiting for your friend to arrive. Or you may have been the one to walk in to your own surprise birthday party. Can you remember how you felt when you heard the noise, ate the cake, and saw the familiar faces of people you love and who love you?

The story line of God's involvement in history, with its many twists and turns, also surprises us. His story builds slowly toward the full revelation of His character and promises. The ending contains a twist that even the most intelligent and insightful can't fully fathom. At the end of human history, Jesus has some surprises for us. He'll come back to wage war against evil and quell the rebellion and hostility against Him. Another intriguing fact is that He has another name—one that has never been revealed before.

God's plan for humanity is a grand one. We won't be disappointed because He's assured us that He will win the battle against all the forces aligned against Him. Whatever the unrevealed name turns out to be, believers in Jesus and the beings in heaven will recognize Jesus as the conquering Hero. What is also amazing is that each believer will also receive a new name (Revelation 2:17).

Question for Today: Where in your life do you need Christ's conquering power?

Prayer: Oh Christ, You are so much more than I can comprehend. I'm curious about Your name that only You know. Even if You never reveal its true meaning, I know You are my Lord and Savior, and You are helping me wage war against all the defeating things in my life. I want victory in You.

Word of God
Finally Victory!

He is dressed in a robe dipped in blood, and his
name is the Word of God (Revelation 19:13).

FYI: This is the only time in the Bible Jesus is named "Word of God," although He is referred to as "the Word" in John 1:1-3.

Someday God will unleash His holy judgment on evil. Rebellious nations will align with Satan and his forces for a titanic battle, the magnitude of which the world has never witnessed. Our heavenly Champion who will defeat them is called "Faithful and True" and another name that no one knows except Him (Revelation 19:1-12).

Faithful and True has another name: "Word of God." Jesus is the revelation and fulfillment of the message of God to the world. Throughout Scripture, God warns people that rejecting His mercy and rebelling against Him will result in paying a terrible price. At the end of time as we know it, the Word of God will lead His heavenly army and destroy His enemies. The first time Jesus came to Earth, His robe was splattered with blood from the beatings He received. The second time He comes, His robe will be stained with the blood of the unrighteous. Sin brings death; repentance brings God's mercy.

We can thank our God that when we submit to His Lordship, we're no longer counted among His enemies. Instead, we become His beloved children.

Question for Today: Are you trusting Jesus for victory over the temptations that get you down?

Prayer: Word of God, I praise You for Your mighty power and ultimate victory over evil.

Lamb
When Is a Lamb Not a Lamb?

The angel showed me the river of the water of
life, as clear as crystal, flowing from the throne
of God and of the Lamb (Revelation 22:1).

FYI: The "throne of God" is also mentioned in Hebrews 12:2; Revelation 7:15; 22:3. All four references reveal that God in heaven rules supreme over everything. The name "Lamb," referring to Jesus, is given 30 times in the New Testament, and all of them are found in Revelation. He is also called the Passover Lamb in Mark 14:12. Luke 22:7, and 1 Corinthians 5:7.

When people say they behave one way, but you believe they really behave another way, you can use the "Duck Test": If it walks like a duck, quacks like a duck, and looks like a duck—it must be a duck. If they say they are good people, but you've observed their habitual bad behaviors, you know they aren't being honest.

The Bible puts that saying on its head with the "Lamb Test": If it doesn't behave like a lamb, doesn't sound like a lamb, and doesn't look like a lamb—it is still the Lamb. A lamb is a docile and defenseless animal that needs constant protection and guidance. The first time Jesus came to Earth, He was a sacrificial Lamb on our behalf. He was "led like a sheep to the slaughter" (Acts 8:32). The second time, He will come as the triumphant Lamb. In the book of Revelation, chapter 22, Jesus is pictured as the all-powerful Lamb sitting on His throne next to the throne of God, with "the river of the water of life...flowing from the throne of God and of the Lamb" (verse 1).

Jesus will valiantly conquer His enemies and throw His archenemy, Satan, into the lake of fire. The Lamb is pictured as having seven horns and seven eyes (Revelation 5:6). He will open the seals on the scroll of God's wrath (Revelation 6). He is the Shepherd of a great multitude of people and marries His bride, the church (Revelation 7:17; 19:7-9). He is so glorious that there is no need for the sun because He lights up the city of God (Revelation 21:23).

Is this the description of a lamb? Absolutely not. In every conceivable way, Christ has turned the world's way of thinking and acting upside down. Today and every day, let's bow down before the majestic Lamb and obey His commands.

Question for Today: How do you worship the Lamb?

Prayer: Magnificent Lamb, You are unlike anything or anyone in the history of the universe. You break all the preconceived notions people have about You. I humbly submit to You and worship You. I praise Your powerful name.

Morning Star
Guarantor of a New Universe

*I, Jesus, have sent my angel to give you this testimony for
the churches. I am the Root and the Offspring of David,
and the bright Morning Star (Revelation 22:16).*

FYI: This is the only time "Morning Star" appears in reference to Jesus.
Peter says we need to pay attention "until the day dawns and the
morning star rises in your hearts" (2 Peter 1:19). Satan is called the
morning star, but he is the instigator of evil and death (Isaiah 14:12-15).

Go outside and look into the heavens. Do you know which star is the
brightest? Obviously the sun. How about the second brightest one?
Though it's not really a star (it's a planet), Venus is bright enough to be seen
at midday and is often visible long after sunset. From ancient times, Venus
has been called the "morning star" because at certain times of the year it's
clearly visible before the sun rises. Since it precedes the sun's appearance,
it acts like a predictor for the coming day.

In the last chapter of the Bible, Revelation 22, Jesus reveals two new
names for Himself. First, He is the "Root and Offspring of David," meaning He brought forth David from obscurity to make him the greatest king
of Israel, and He will fulfill God's promise to David that one of his descendants will sit on his throne forever (1 Kings 2:45; Isaiah 9:7). He will fulfill that promise when He defeats His enemies, who will be thrown into
the lake of fire (Revelation 20:11-15).

Then something happens that is beyond our imagination. The whole
universe as we know it will be destroyed, and a new heaven and a new
earth will be created (Isaiah 65:17; 2 Peter 3:13; Revelation 21:1). Jesus calls
Himself the bright Morning Star. He will brilliantly herald God's new creation. Much better than the planet Venus, Jesus is the guarantor of everything new that God has planned for His people.

Worship and adore the Morning Star of a whole new universe!

Question for Today: Are you allowing the bright Morning Star to shine in your heart?

Prayer: Morning Star, shine brilliantly in my life, and rise supremely in my heart. Fill me with Your love, compassion, strength, and wisdom. I want to reflect Your glory each day.

Bibliography

Lockyer, Herbert, *All the Divine Names and Titles in the Bible* (Grand Rapids, MI: Zondervan Publishing, 1988).

Purnell, Dick, *Knowing God by His Names* (Eugene, OR: Harvest House Publishers, 2005).

Smith, F. LaGard, *The Narrated Bible* (Eugene, OR: Harvest House Publishers, 1999).

Spangler, Ann, *Names of God Bible* (Grand Rapids, MI: Fleming H. Revell, 2011).

Tenney, Merrill C., *Zondervan Pictorial Bible Dictionary* (Grand Rapids, MI: Zondervan, 1963).

About Dick Purnell

Through his books and humorous personal speaking style, Dick Purnell has encouraged people all over the world to develop a close personal relationship with the Lord. He has spoken to audiences in all 50 states in America, as well as thirteen other countries. He and his wife, Paula, have been senior speakers for nineteen years at FamilyLife's Weekend to Remember marriage conferences.

Besides his bestselling book *Knowing God by His Names*, Dick has authored 18 other books, including *Growing Closer to God, Making a Good Marriage Even Better, Discovering God's Unique Purpose for You* and the award-winning *Becoming a Friend and Lover*.

Dick earned a master's degree in education from Indiana University and a master's degree in theology from Trinity International University. He has been on the staff of Cru for more than 30 years.

To receive information about bringing him to speak to your retreat, conference, church or special event, contact Dick at (919) 363-8000. Visit his website at www.dickpurnell.com.

To learn more about Harvest House books and
to read sample chapters, visit our website:

www.harvesthousepublishers.com

HARVEST HOUSE PUBLISHERS
EUGENE, OREGON
